Answers for Modern Communicators

This book provides students and professionals with practical answers to important career and communication questions, helping them to communicate successfully in a business setting. Communication expert, Deirdre Breakenridge, examines the ways in which professionals can make the most of their careers in a fast-changing media landscape, offering advice on how new and seasoned executives can utilize and adapt to the latest modes of communication.

The author breaks down the eight most critical areas for professionals seeking to develop their communication skills, opening with essentials that will prove useful in any setting. She then details the ways in which organizations can adapt to changes in technology and consumer behavior to improve relationships, social media presence, and brand recognition. The easy to follow question–answer format walks readers through the most pressing, confusing, and frequently asked questions about successful communication with plenty of advice and examples for a better learning experience. Covering traditional business communication topics like partnerships and storytelling, the book also includes material on digital and social media channels as well as a chapter on giving back as a mentor. "Experts Weigh In" boxes feature advice from other top professionals, exposing the reader to multiple perspectives from the field.

Grounded in decades of experience, *Answers for Modern Communicators* will benefit all students getting ready to enter the workforce as well as professionals looking to enhance their communication skills.

Deirdre Breakenridge is Chief Executive Officer of Pure Performance Communications, USA, a firm that provides strategic communications consulting for building effective integrated marketing, public relations, and social media programs. She also teaches social media and PR classes at the University of Massachusetts—Amherst, USA and is a LinkedIn Learning Instructor with video courses in PR and marketing.

"Packed with insights and real-life examples, Breakenridge's new book offers the best answers to PR professionals' many questions about our industry and how it's evolving. Breakenridge is a highly sought after strategist and thought-leader, a podcaster, author, professor, and Lynda.com instructor. She shares her considerable knowledge and expertise in a conversational style that makes you feel like she's talking directly to you."

Martin Waxman,
Martin Waxman Communications and Seneca College,
Canada

"As I was reading *Answers for Modern Communicators* by my friend and colleague Deirdre Breakenridge, the all-too-familiar childhood refrain, "Curiosity killed the cat," kept running through my head. How many of us in our younger years found ourselves being admonished sternly by our elders when we persisted with our, "Who? What? When? Where? Why?" questions?!? And how many of us have found ourselves either working for someone who had no idea what comprises effective communication or have ourselves been at a loss for words when asked "What exactly *is* it that you do?"

As Deirdre says as she starts this excellent 'all the questions you should be able to answer' guide, "Asking questions helps you learn the essentials of your profession. The answers are critical to your role as a successful communicator."

After all, you wouldn't want to find yourself in the position of Alice in Lewis Carroll's *Alice in Wonderland* who, when asked by the Cheshire Cat where she wanted to go, responded, "I don't much care where." To which the Cat promptly retorted, "Then it doesn't matter which way you go."

Not only does Deirdre present the *questions* that every communicator should be asking, she also presents the rationale for *asking* those questions... how a deeper understanding of your profession can help you serve your client or employer more effectively and efficiently. *Answers for Modern Communicators* helps you understand the pathways that are available to you for communicating and the value that each can bring to your communication initiatives. As I say so often to my students and others, 'Read and heed!'"

Kirk Hazlett,
APR, Fellow, PRSA, Curry College,
USA

"*Answers for Modern Communicators* would have been a game-changer for me when I made the shift from journalism to corporate communications. The review copy I received so I could write this testimonial has already proven useful. Why nobody has approached a primer to communications as a Q&A based on the obvious questions any communicator might ask at various stages of their careers is beyond me. As if Deirdre's straightforward, common-sense answers aren't enough, she has added observations from some of the smartest professionals around who are best-suited to address specific questions. I'd like to say this book deserves a spot on every communicator's bookshelf, but it won't stay on the shelf for long. Unlike most read-it-once business books, it is bound to become a dog-eared reference volume."

Shel Holtz,
Principal at Holtz Communication + Technology,
USA

Answers for Modern Communicators

A Guide to Effective Business Communication

Deirdre Breakenridge

Routledge
Taylor & Francis Group
NEW YORK AND LONDON

First published 2018
by Routledge
711 Third Avenue, New York, NY 10017

and by Routledge
2 Park Square, Milton Park, Abingdon, Oxon, OX14 4RN

Routledge is an imprint of the Taylor & Francis Group, an informa business

Library of Congress Cataloging-in-Publication Data
A catalog record for this book has been requested

ISBN: 978-1-138-71443-4 (hbk)
ISBN: 978-0-415-30392-7 (pbk)
ISBN: 978-1-315-23075-7 (ebk)

Typeset in Palatino
by Sunrise Setting Ltd, Brixham, UK

Contents

Figures

Foreword

How do you equip yourself with the skills for a future you don't yet know? It's a question that's challenging organizations around the world.

The pace of change in the media, marketing, and public relations is frenzied. You need to have a positive attitude to learning and development if you want to stay ahead.

In my day job at Ketchum, I run an engagement community of around 600 people worldwide. We track significant changes in media and technology related to public relations practice and typically share 30 to 50 updates with the business each month.

It would be a full-time job for an individual to have an expert knowledge in every area of digital or social media practice. This is just one of many areas of modern public relations.

Time served is the typical measure of competence, but not all experience is equal and when media and technology are changing so quickly, it's a lousy metric.

Foundation knowledge, however, is a powerful tool. Each career step forward that I've taken has been preceded by a period of formal training or coaching. It's no accident.

Professional frameworks set out the skills you need at each stage of your career. They are the foundations for learning and development.

In more mature professions, such as finance and law, competency is linked directly to earnings. In other sectors, such as public relations and digital marketing, it's a work in progress.

Setting personal goals and matching learning and training activities is a good way to ensure that you stay ahead. I track my Continuous Professional Development (CPD) via the Chartered Institute of Public Relations (CIPR).

Logging your development via a professional association isn't the only way to ensure that you develop your skills but it's a good discipline. Setting personal goals and matching learning and training activities is a good way to ensure that you stay ahead.

The day that you stop learning is the day you should stop practicing.

Ketchum has a small team worldwide focused on learning and development, and helping our business make sense of the market for education.

We're continually upskilling the agency by moving from formal classroom learning to social learning platforms, from workshops to webinars, and from one-off sessions to continuous learning.

This year 1,600 client-facing practitioners have completed five online courses via a social learning platform aimed at ensuring that the business keeps its skills and talent up to scratch.

The most powerful learning tool I've got is the community that I have developed around my blog. It's people that I'm connected with via Facebook, LinkedIn, and Twitter.

They're the people I ask for help and turn to for inspiration.

During the last few years we've characterized the third-party tool market, explored mental health, and examined the relationship between research and practice in public relations.

We've crowdsourced a guide to public speaking, developed a framework to tackle fake news, and explored ways of tackling writer's block.

Deirdre has done a wonderful and very generous thing in creating *Answers for Modern Communicators* – she's shared her knowledge and her own personal community with us.

In each chapter, Deirdre shares responses to questions that she's been asked in recent years. And along the way, she introduces us to some of her mentors.

My grandfather was my greatest mentor. He taught me the most powerful means of learning. He had a natural curiosity and an enthusiasm that was infectious.

Whatever you do and however you learn, throw yourself into it.

Stephen Waddington is Partner and Chief Engagement Officer at Ketchum, helping clients and colleagues to do the best job possible engaging with the public. He is responsible for driving the integration of digital and social capabilities in client engagements across the agency's international network.

He is Visiting Professor in Practice at the Newcastle University, supporting the university and students through teaching and mentoring.

Stephen was President of the CIPR in 2014, during which time he helped return the organization to its roots of professionalism as set out in its Royal Charter. He is a Chartered PR Practitioner, a CIPR Fellow (Hon.), and member of the City of London Public Relations Guild and PRCA.

Acknowledgements

What a wonderful journey I've traveled in communications ... 25+ years and counting. I've experienced some of the best years of my life in PR and marketing. My first—and my longest—mentor, Fraser Seitel, who is author of *The Practice of Public Relations* and the President of Emerald Partners, has guided me in so many ways over the years. I don't know where to begin when it comes to giving thanks to Fraser. He helped me to secure my first internship back in 1986 with Padilla Spear Burdick and Beardsley in New York City. In 2012, it was also Fraser who introduced me to PR and communications veteran, John Doorley, who at the time was the Program Director for the School of Professional Studies at NYU. Within two weeks, I was preparing a syllabus to teach at NYU as an Adjunct Professor. John has also fueled my growth. My experience at NYU helped me to move my teaching to a whole new level, sharing ideas with very smart graduate students from around the world. I'm a firm believer in reverse mentoring. Teaching at NYU is the perfect example of two-way learning.

There are many professionals in my life who stand out. It would be difficult to name them all. From the colleagues in my #PRStudChat Twitter community who share their advice openly and on a daily basis, to other colleagues I've met through NYU, Rutgers, and UMASS. They've helped me to become a better educator and communications professional. Of course, to my professional peers who have gone above and beyond to help me with this book, I want to thank them from the bottom of my heart. A big thank you, Ai Zhang, Ai Ching Goh, Aliza Licht, Corina Manea, Dorie Clark, Gail Nelson, Gini Dietrich, Heather Whaling, Jennifer Connelly, Joe Provenza, Karen Freberg, Leta Soza, Michael Ehrlich, Nathan Burgess, Neal Schaffer, Peter Shankman, Priya Ramesh, Rebekah Iliff, Richard Bistrong, Sandra Fathi, Shonali Burke, Stephanie Carls, Valerie Simon, Wendy Glavin, and Steven Waddington for writing my book Foreword. You have all enriched my career and my life.

The principles, lessons, advice, and insights you have shared are invaluable.

I also have to give a shout out and thank you to Jess Ostroff for creating her company, Don't Panic Management (DPM). If it wasn't for DPM and Kimberly Voorhis, my Virtual Assistant (VA), I would never have been able to write this book and manage everything else that was going on in my career. Thank you, Jess and Kimberly, for always having my back and keeping me so incredibly organized.

When *Answers for Modern Communicators* started to take shape, I began searching for the right publisher. I was introduced to my Routledge team and I'm so thankful for the guidance, support, and collaboration they provided. Sharon Golan and Erin Arata have helped me to construct and mold the pages of this book.

I also want to thank my designer, Lilla Bardenova, who created the illustrations for *Answers for Modern Communicators*. Lilla had less than a month to create the graphics. She delivered with speed and creativity, capturing my vision and nailing all the designs.

As for my family, I want to thank them for their constant love and support. Publishing a book is an exciting accomplishment. But it can also be stressful throughout the process. Thankfully, my family was there through all the highs and right there next to me during the lows. They have helped me to stay focused, grounded, and always on the right track. I am truly blessed!

Lastly, I want to thank all my PR, marketing, and social media friends around the world. Thank you for all your questions and answers and the thoughts you share with me through email, Facebook, LinkedIn, Skype, and Twitter. You are an amazing source of inspiration and for you I have written this book.

Introduction

Every Modern Communicator Has a Question

When I started my journey in public relations and marketing, no one said to me, "Deirdre, it is time to give back." As you learn, grow, and feel confident in your career, you naturally want to pass along information to your colleagues and peers. I've built an entire career helping business professionals to communicate more effectively. Along the way, mentoring and teaching came naturally and have always been top of my mind. But, I never felt as if I had to mentor; I just wanted to give back. At the same time, I quickly learned that everyone has a question and everyone wants to be a good modern communicator. As you can only imagine, mentoring has become a daily exchange of Q&A.

Thinking back to the late 1990s, mentoring was a much more formal relationship. As a former communications agency owner, I used to work with employees, teaching them their roles, responsibilities, and the skills necessary to succeed in the agency environment and with their client accounts. My goal was to teach them the business of communication. There were times when I felt like a mom, "raising" many of them and navigating through the tough times, as if they were my own kids. I also enjoyed interacting with one or two young professionals outside of the office. They were my official "mentees." We would meet once a week for coffee, or catch up by telephone. Several of these young professionals would shadow me, experiencing a day in the life of a communicator.

Today, mentoring has expanded exponentially, helping professionals to make the most of their careers in a crazy, fast-changing media landscape. Keeping up with the times or the trends is not easy. You have to stay on top of consumer media consumption habits and how businesses must adapt to social media and new technologies across their organizations. Even though I'm a professor mentoring students in the online classroom, I also mentor professionals through LinkedIn messages, answer questions publicly on Twitter (via @dbreakenridge), and share advice privately through Facebook messaging. I video Skype with students from universities around the world, sometimes a couple of times a week. I don't know these students well, but I see their ambition and aspirations through our social media conversations.

Realizing I'm 25+ years into my career, I had to figure out an even bigger way to give back. I thought the best approach would be to select the most meaningful and challenging questions I have been asked throughout the years and share the answers or the lessons I have learned, all packaged neatly into a book. *Answers for Modern Communicators* breaks down the most important areas for communicators who want to learn and excel with their modern communication skills. Each chapter has helpful Q&A with the most pressing, concerning, confusing, and frequently asked questions, with advice and examples for a better learning experience.

The advice I offer you is the information that has kept me focused and on track as a communicator for many years. *Answers for Modern Communicators* is my way of answering important career and communication-focused queries and imparting advice that spans decades. The goal is to make a difference in the lives of my professionals and peers, and to help you, the modern communicator, wherever you are in the world. After all, the best learning takes place through your own experience and the experience of others.

Answers for Modern Communicators is also a way for me to mentor many people all at once and in a more in-depth manner. I wanted to respond to the questions that flow through my Twitter feed daily, come to me via my LinkedIn inbox, and show up on Facebook from students and professionals around the world, who are searching for their answers. When one person has a question, this means a thousand more may have the very same question. I offer my answers to questions at the front of every chapter. There is also guidance at the end of each chapter from many of my influential marketing friends. They, too, provide their best advice, all to help shape your course as a modern communicator.

In Chapter 1, "Learning the Essentials," you'll find the absolute essentials or communication survival skills; what I learned early on and then "lived," regardless of the many ongoing changes in technology, consumer behavior, and the evolving media landscape. The essentials mold the communicator to handle a number of situations and to be a savvier and seasoned professional, no matter how many years of experience they have.

The foundation of any business is built on solid relationships and trust. Relationships come and go, but the questions and answers shared in Chapter 2, "Growing Relationships Built to Last," are based on building relationships that have the potential to develop and grow over time. The questions and answers included in the chapter are focused on business and relationships with constituents, even when facing tough situations and numerous obstacles. The lessons are personal experiences, as I was cultivating important friendships and partnerships for the long term.

Chapter 3, "Socializing Your Brand," is one of the big turning points for modern communicators. As a "traditional" PR pro who started in a small agency, I was typing media lists and news releases on a Brother typewriter. I was also using a fax machine to send those very same releases to news departments across the country. The fax machine was the "hot" technology of the time. The answers to the questions in this chapter focus on getting you up to speed with technology and social media; what it will take for you to embrace an evolving media landscape. The advice and stories are a good reminder that you have to chart a technology course. However, you should never lose sight of the people who are at the heart of your business and what it means to deliver valuable communication to them through new media channels.

In Chapter 4, "Taking Your Stories to the Next Level," the questions and answers are presented for modern communicators who know it is time to change the art of storytelling. But, you may not know how or feel confident enough to take bold steps. Not only do you have to embrace the best of storytelling from the past; you also have to incorporate new thinking and unique ways to capture attention with content, driving interest and engagement. Modern communicators benefit from real-time experiences that focus on the techniques that move you from average so-so stories to making an impact through all your communication outreach.

Chapter 5, "Owning Your Brand and Your Reputation," offers advice focused on the importance of building and owning a good professional brand. Whether you are a young professional just starting out or a seasoned veteran, you will be evaluated regardless of your small or vast digital footprint. As a modern communicator, you will learn to create a strong professional brand, understanding the importance of monitoring media properties carefully. Your brand is what you stand for and the answers in this chapter reinforce what it takes to build, maintain, and protect your brand.

Chapter 6, "Measuring Your Success," is an extremely personal area. The experiences shared will be interpreted differently by everyone who reads this book. Why? Because success is different for each and every one of us. At the same time, a business must nail down goals and clearly identify what success looks like. This chapter shares what has influenced my career and journey, from the greatest success to the lessons learned about creating value in the business environment. In Chapter 6, the Q&A will guide you and help you to gauge success that is tailored specifically for you and your organization.

It took me about ten years in to "officially" mentor. However, it might take you less time. Chapter 7, "Giving Back as a Mentor", will help you to understand how and when to mentor, the best tips for mentoring and some extra lessons that will assist you in your own career. Even the best mentors need career-long mentoring. You are never too young or too old to be mentored. The answers shared in this chapter come from my own career journey, applying what my mentors have taught me over the years; the sage advice that has stayed the course for decades. The Q&A also represents some of the most frequently asked questions I have received and enjoyed answering for my mentees.

The last chapter in the book wraps up all the questions and answers to guide the modern communicator. Of course, there will always be more questions, answers, challenges, and opportunities as a result. When you are curious and push yourself out of your comfort zone to try new experiences and to learn from others, you will find greater rewards. *Answers for Modern Communicators* offers you new ideas and a stronger foundation to excel in your career and as a mentor. Every answer to a question has the potential to influence your own course, help you find new opportunities for yourself and your organization, and help someone else in a different and positive way.

Are you ready be a modern communicator? Do you want to chart a new course? Good luck on your journey. As you create new experiences, be sure to ask more questions to enhance your learning and answer as many questions as you can for your peers who need your help.

Chapter 1

Learning the Essentials

Early in my career, I remember wishing there was a resource or some type of guide with answers to the strategic, yet "in the trenches," questions and answers that a communication professional faces on a daily basis. There are a lot of good books on the subjects of PR, marketing, social media, and how integrated communication affects a business. But, where are the essentials, or the "do this" and you better not "do that" guidance to survive as a modern communicator today? Do you have all the answers you need to your most pressing questions?

Sometimes you have questions and you don't know how to phrase them or you don't know who to ask. What about the dreaded "stupid" question? Did you ever have one of those? A question that is considered outside of the normal scope or just doesn't fit what someone would expect you to ask? People have asked me publicly and privately, and pretty much daily, the questions that run the "communication gamut" and beyond. Now, I am sharing them with you. In my experience there are no stupid questions; maybe just "stupid" answers when people don't really listen to what you're saying or truly understand what you need.

Asking questions helps you to learn the essentials of your profession. The answers are critical to your role as a successful modern communicator. So, don't ever stop asking your questions. Simultaneously, you need to gain access to many crucial practices and to have personal stories at your fingertips. When you are on the job, on your feet, or faced with an urgent situation, you'll want to have quick answers to essential questions on hand and in an instant. No time to think or to research on Google. You have to move forward and know how to get your job done. One of the best ways to tap into the essentials is by learning through another professional's experience.

Being a student in the physical classroom gave me a great foundation of knowledge. I wouldn't trade my years at Glassboro State College (now Rowan University) or my MBA at Fairleigh

Dickinson University (FDU) for anything. But today your classroom is everywhere, and you should take advantage of this … in person, online, and through social media. At the same time, it was my positions with different companies, the experiences and interactions with supervisors and my peers, and the wisdom of colleagues and mentors, that truly guided me. It all started with many, many questions. They say curiosity is a sign of leadership. Perhaps this is why many parents believe that their kids, by the age of three, will be natural leaders. The answers to those questions help carve the path to career development and personal growth.

Based on all my own questions over the years and the many questions I have been asked, here is a set of essential questions and answers for you to use and practice. These answers are the Frequently Asked Questions (FAQs), on the job and in the trenches. Now, you don't have to worry about the stupid questions or wait for someone else to ask what you really need to know. Best of all … no more guessing.

Question 1. Why Should You Learn Your Company's Business Inside and Out?

Absorb as much information as you can about your own organization and your marketplace. Learning the business, and really showing an interest in your company beyond your own responsibilities, leads to more opportunities and will make you stand out.

I applied this advice early on in my career. As a result, I was invited into the boardroom with the senior executives at my agency. Did I enjoy reading those financial newspapers and industrial equipment trade publications? Well, not in the beginning but they certainly grew on me in time. Why did I read them? Because professionals who want to excel must know their own businesses and/or their clients' businesses as if they were their own. These pros can speak intelligently to any audience, especially the media. You can become a valuable resource for a journalist/blogger just by being able to answer company questions directly and in less time.

Here are a few ways for you to learn the business inside and out:

1. Scour the company's trade publications or magazines related to your industry.
2. Watch the news program for a worldly view of what affects your company's industry and the marketplace.
3. Set up your Google Alerts to know when your company is mentioned online and in the news.
4. Ask to receive marketing and sales bulletins and other internal department publications at your company.
5. Find out what your CEO reads from his/her executive assistant, then add those publications to your reading list.
6. Find out what your supervisors are reading and take the time to get a subscription or set up an RSS feed.
7. Listen to podcast shows that focus on topics related to your industry.
8. Learn from the well-known bloggers in your industry and engage in any online events and conversations for more knowledge.

When you learn your company's business, you will also interact on a much higher level with executives, customers, partners, and other important constituents.

Question 2. Why Is It Important to Speak Less and to Listen More?

I know many communicators who have the gift of conversation. They are incredibly interesting, but there is never a moment of silence when you're in their presence. You must always know when to stop talking. The best communicators try to curtail their own communication to listen more to the people around them. It's not always about what message you want to communicate. Your time to share will definitely come.

Whether you're in the personal or professional setting, you should not be "listening" just to formulate your next sentence. How do you know when someone is really paying attention? Here are a few signs of the true listener:

1. Active listeners will make eye contact with you.
2. Active listeners will be able to repeat back what you say in their answers.
3. Active listeners will ask follow-up questions.
4. Active listeners will engage with their interest and their intellect.
5. Active listeners turn out to be the best conversationalists.

At the same time, you can also tell when someone is not listening. They give you a vacant stare as they are framing how they want to present their own information. Plus, their responses are representative of some kind of pre-set agenda.

Instead of focusing on your own points and getting your message across, practice speaking less, and listening more with an acute ear. If you do, then you'll be absorbing critical information that you can use and, better yet, act upon. With this approach, you will gain a greater understanding of what people need from you, and why they take the time to share information with you in the first place.

When the time comes, you will share your messages. And, if you listen first and share second, then the chances of what you say being well received will increase tenfold. Why? The reason is simple. The knowledge you gather and what you have learned from listening will show in your own communication.

Figure 1.1 Active Listening

Question 3. If You Practice PR, Then Are You Considered a Marketer?

If you don't understand how or why PR fits into a larger marketing framework, then you can only be partially effective in your role. PR has become a crucial part of any marketing program. PR builds the brand awareness, trust, credibility, and advocacy through media and relationships with key constituents. PR helps to optimize the company's marketing efforts, including your advertising, promotions, digital marketing, social media, etc.

If PR and marketing are working together, then all your communication is consistent in messaging, design, and experience. Your consumers want to receive the same great brand experience, at every touch point with your company. This can only happen when PR and marketing are on the same page and operating in synch with one another. The customer doesn't ask, "Who sent me this communication? Was it PR or was it marketing?"

Working together as a team of communicators is not a new experience. Back in the days before digital and social media opened up new communication channels, PR and marketing had to coordinate together. For example, at my old agency, marketers and PR pros worked on the precise timing of messages in their print feature stories and product reviews, balanced out by brand and product advertising in trade publications. You would see the same consistent messaging show up in editorial stories as you did in advertisements, although the third-party endorsement was far more powerful. Plus, PR paved the way to credibility so that advertising would help maintain awareness and drive sales. What started back in the days before the Internet is even more pronounced today.

PR and marketing should be shoulder-to-shoulder and arm-in-arm, as comrades. You can't have one without the other. Embrace your togetherness as a communication team. If you're in PR, then you're in marketing too.

Question 4. Why Should You Keep Ethics Top of Mind?

Trust your instincts. If you feel you're going to communicate news or company information that is causing you to take pause, then stop and speak up. Ask yourself, "Is what I'm about to disclose lacking truth, fairness, or accuracy and does it benefit all of the people I'm trying to reach?" Even if it is your boss or a supervisor who has given you a directive, go with your gut feelings. At times, you may have to challenge other professionals, and change the communication, or make the decision not to participate in a program.

Skilled communicators understand the serious ramifications of unethical communication including the legal ramifications. You have to be familiar with the meaning of ethical conduct. Organizations, such as the Public Relations Society of America (PRSA), share a Code of Ethics to help break down ethical communication for you. The International Association of Business Communicators (IABC) also has a Global Standard, which includes the highest standards of professional behavior.

My friend and colleague, Kirk Hazlett, APR, Fellow PRSA, summed up the importance of ethics in a blog post discussing PRSA Ethics Month. He said,

> September is traditionally the time of the year when the Public Relations Society of America observes "Ethics Month," and PRSA chapters nationwide are encouraged to present special programming. A comprehensive set of resources is available to assist in this effort. While I support and encourage this educational emphasis, both on a *personal* and a *professional* level, I would prefer to see it a year-round, continuous initiative.[1]

The bottom line—ethical conduct is an everyday practice because every day it is your reputation that could be at stake. Professionally and personally, no one can demand you do something that makes you feel uncomfortable. You create your own actions and you are ultimately responsible. At the end of the day, all you have left is your integrity. If you put yourself in a compromising situation, then you risk tarnishing your own reputation and your credibility as a professional.

Question 5. Do You Have to Audit Your Communications?

Moving forward with more precise and meaningful communication means you understand what has been done and what has worked well in the past. Knowing the history gives you a better chance to achieve success, and to avoid any failed efforts. Before you communicate, ask yourself, "Do I have a comprehensive understanding of the big picture, and what has worked well and what has not?" Having the answer to this question is a "fix it to move forward" approach. After all, why move forward with problems from the past that will just continue to hinder your progress?

Here's where auditing your communication initiatives and uncovering your strengths and weaknesses come into play. You should be asking questions about what you've said and done in the past, and whether your efforts have been effective or not.

These questions may include:

- Are your communications aligned with your organizational goals?
- Are you integrating your marketing efforts across your organization?
- Are you taking full advantage of your communication channels?
- Are your communication channels operating efficiently and effectively?
- Who are your different target audiences and do you have communication tailored to each group?
- Have you developed consistent, clear and concise messages for all audiences?
- Do you know how your audience wants to receive information from you?

However, two more important questions, which should always be top of mind, are: "What do your customers think of your communication?" and "What would make your communication with them more effective?" These questions are frequently overlooked, but lead to more precise communication and achieving your goals. If you can learn what customers want from you, then you will be able to help them much more in the future.

Best of all, today, you don't have to wait until your program is over to audit and then apply the fix part to propel forward with a greater purpose. You can gather information and feedback from your customers through data in real time and at different intervals. Social media data, website analytics, performance analytics, and automated CRM (Customer Relations Management) software help you to fix what's broken and to adjust quickly and accordingly.

So, yes, audit your programs for background information and extract what did and did not work. Then, fix your issues and move forward with your customers' needs at the forefront. These are the key steps and they provide a better way of learning and increasing the effectiveness of your communications.

Question 6. Why Is Knowing the News Always Your Business?

Reading about current events is a must for every communicator. My mentor shared this advice with me 25 years ago, and I'm still practicing it daily. At the time, he told me to select one or two publications and read them every day. Perhaps you might choose *The New York Times*, the *Wall Street Journal*, or CNN.com, or you may prefer USA Today. Make local, national, and international news your business.

At the same time, read the PR, marketing, advertising, and social media publications to stay up to date with industry news and challenges facing the profession. *PR Week*, PR News, *Adweek* and *Advertising Age* are good, go-to sources. Top blogs with the latest news and helpful marketing and PR tips include Spin Sucks, PR Expanded (personal plug, this is my blog), PR Daily, PRSay, CommPRO, Convince & Convert, and Social Media Examiner. There are far too many to list. You can find more of the top marketing and PR blogs, for example, at Alltop.com, under "Topics" and "PR." Bookmark these blog sites.

Then, for the communicators who are constantly on the go, and want the quicker highlights on current events, there are daily quick news fixes. For example, the Skimm gives you just the right amount of information every morning to get you through the day, with links to more details on a variety of news stories. The Huffington Post also has daily news briefs, with links to national and world news, keeping communicators well versed in business, politics, media, tech, and entertainment topics. What about news apps on your smartphone? From cable TV and network news apps to curated and customized headlines from Newsbeat or Flipbook, your news can always travel along with you. Or, maybe you're listening to your favorite news podcasts including For Immediate Release (FIR) with Shel Holtz and The BeanCast with Bob Knorpp.

Communicators have to be well rounded. You can't expect to sit with the executives at the boardroom table if you're not up on your news and industry information. Plus, in my experience, you never know when small talk at events or social gatherings on important issues can open doors to exciting new relationships and opportunities in business.

If you are trying to be a part of the business or helping to grow the business, then you have to make the news your business.

Question 7. What Exactly Is PR and How Does It Bring Value to a Business?

As a modern communicator, you have to know and be able to explain public relations. Here's one of my most frequently asked questions: "What do PR people really do?" My best friend's mom, who's known me for almost 20 years, just asked this question. She's not the only one. Most industry definitions of PR discuss how professionals build "mutually beneficial relationships" through strategic communication.[2] True, but a broad definition.

What does PR mean to me? How do I use communication to create meaning? How does my outreach lead to value for different groups of people and, most of all, build relationships? In the business world, when you make PR a part of your communications program, you quickly learn the real-world definition. The "P" stands for "Personal" and the "R" translates into "Relationships" that are built by sharing targeted, meaningful communication and becoming a trusted source. Words like "mass" or "broadcast messaging," "spin," and "hype" should not be a part of your vocabulary or your thinking.

At the same time, PR helps to interpret how different groups perceive, and respond to, your communication. When you're in PR you also evaluate what actions result. A career in PR means you will be instrumental in creating the communication that:

1. shifts an opinion;
2. changes behavior;
3. builds reputation;
4. builds the bridges of understanding between the people you connect.

Of course, if you don't deliver meaning and value with your communication, then you will not reach the best part of PR; what it is like to be the trusted source, creating strong relationships with many different constituents, including the media.

Now that you know PR, you can help spread the word about the meaning and value of PR.

Question 8. How Do You Score High on the Ethics Test?

Companies are in the news daily and they are called out on social media as a result of their unethical conduct. Not just the big companies, from a specific industry, but companies of all sizes and organizations doing business in every market. Scandals range from diversity issues and sexual harassment to fraudulent accounting practices and communication missteps via social media.

What would you do if you were asked to provide counsel on a matter that you believed was unethical? Would you want to be on the PR team if you knew about a potential "cover-up," with a deliberate lack of openness about a situation that negatively affected your customers? What would you have done if you were the communicators on the job when Enron, Arthur Andersen, AIG, BP, etc., were under scrutiny and not completely transparent in their communications? What about the political campaign surrogates in the 2016 Presidential election who went on TV for all the world to see and said anything to support their candidates? Would you stand behind someone if you knew that they were stretching the truth or outright lying? These are all ethical questions that only you can answer.

Your answers will depend on whether you believe in the behavior that has occurred, and if you feel you're representing the truth. Ask yourself, "Am I representing the *truth*?" If you know there is a cover-up in play, or you suspect the company's actions are unethical (or a political candidate's actions for that matter), then as an ethical communicator you don't want to further the dishonest conduct.

Always review all your accounts, cases, opportunities, support/volunteer work, and communication carefully. If you remain aware, objective in nature, trust your instincts, expand your perspective, and err on the side of caution, then you will score high on the ethics test. Hopefully, you will influence others to do the same.

Question 9. Should Training Stop When You Are a Seasoned Pro?

Sure, younger professionals need different types of training: speaker, presentation, diversity, management, and leadership. However, so do the seasoned pros. Executives need coaching too. For instance, even the best public speakers require constant practice and critique. Most professionals don't recognize their own poor speaking habits. For example, they're usually the last to figure out that they favor certain pause words. For years, I said the word "again" far too many times, which was a difficult speaking pattern to break. Someone else had to help me kick the habit!

Think about your own speaking and presentation habits when working with different groups. Do you know your annoying pause words (um, wow, so, absolutely, again, to name a few)?

Here is another test for you (or your executives) who think they don't need training:

1. Do you know if your physical stance is uninviting or highly approachable?
2. Would you be able to tell if your communication paints a clear picture or if what you say is confusing?
3. Would you recognize whether your body language was friendly or told a different story?
4. Do you know how to establish a connection with your audience even before you speak?

Be honest ... chances are you may not. Training at intervals in your career helps to make your communication more targeted, vivid, and meaningful to an audience. They say, "Practice makes perfect." But, it should be "practice and frequent training make perfect."

Question 10. Do Executives Need Media Coaching ... Even If They Don't Think So?

Right up there with the important training is ongoing media coaching. Even the most poised and well-spoken C-level executives need help. Sharing information with a journalist for a print or online story is completely different than a TV appearance or a media Skype interview. Then, when crisis strikes, the friendly questions disappear, and issue-related questions become rapid fire. Your executives will be the first to say they don't need training, or "I've been trained in the past." Stand firm on why they do need training (because situations and the media constantly change) and don't back down.

Can you ever be fully prepared for what the media or the public will ask? It's unlikely, but good media training sessions will better prepare you or your executives to answer questions on point and succinctly, in good times and bad. The goal is to deliver the most important and accurate messages in a polished and credible manner. At the same time, it's better to test your media skills before the crisis strikes and not in the midst of a full-blown crisis.

Unfortunately, I've witnessed too many interviews "gone bad." I can immediately tell the difference between the trained company spokesperson and the one who didn't take the time to get more professional practice. You have one shot in an interview to deliver information that will set the record straight, or impart valuable information on behalf of your company.

Remember, when it comes to the media ... there are no do-overs. Please get it right the first time. Good coaching always helps.

Question 11. How Do You Maximize Earned Media Opportunities?

Among all the ways you can create awareness, earned media is considered the most credible. The power of the third-party endorsement carries far more weight than a message crafted and placed in an advertisement or in a digital promotion. When someone else recommends your company, especially someone you trust, the endorsement carries influence, much more than anything you would read directly from the company. Consumers know that advertising, promotions, and other forms of owned and paid media are all carefully orchestrated to capture attention and to create impact.

There are so many opportunities to maximize your earned media efforts through any number of channels today. Third-party endorsements come in many different forms, from your editorial placements and social media comments from fans, to online reviews and customer testimonials on your website. Today, earned media can also be the conversations customers are having about your company and your products in their social media communities—including Facebook, Twitter, Instagram, Yelp, and Reddit—when you're not around.

However, maximizing earned media starts with the company's actions. Businesses have to show they care and that they're focused on serving customers and their other stakeholders. Becoming a better employer, partner, vendor, provider, etc., is the best way to get people talking positively. At the same time, businesses are built on great people. So, it becomes everyone's job to help the business operate at optimal performance. Then, their favorite journalists, bloggers, friends, and customers want to talk favorably about them or recommend their product and service offerings.

When the company does its part internally, then you will see the interest and appreciation grow through earned media with external audiences. When this happens, there is a ripple effect. Other people are much more likely to pay attention and act on the recommendations of the people they trust.

When working from the inside out, you are maximizing your earned media opportunities.

Question 12. Why Is It Important to be Recognized Outside of Your Silo?

There are communication challenges across your entire company. Make it your business to know what keeps the executives up at night. Perhaps these challenges relate to low productivity or poor customer satisfaction. Working in a silo, sectioned off from other areas in the company:

1. will not help you to understand and solve issues; or
2. get you noticed outside of your respective department.

Your ability to work with other teams propels you into new and interesting work. The more you can engage with other areas, including HR, Sales, Legal, Customer Service, etc., the more you'll understand the challenges from a different perspective. You'll be able to offer more realistic solutions to organizational problems. At the same time, sharing, collaborating, and innovating with other groups is the key not only to your own growth and development but also to moving your company to greater success through the synergy of diverse people and teams. Working beyond yourself and your department results in career growth and recognition.

When I interviewed Samantha Paxson, CMO of Co-op Financial Services, on my podcast show, *Women Worldwide*, she shared a story with me about her career growth. Samantha didn't wait for anyone in her company to anoint her as the person to solve problems affecting different departments and ultimately improve delivery for the client. She proactively did this on her own. Samantha knew that if she worked with areas outside of marketing, such as Operations and IT, she would not only immediately stand out, but also solve problems more quickly. She believed that "business happens in the spaces between functions." Long story short, this is how Samantha, by the age of 30, earned the title of Vice President and now is CMO of her company.[3]

If you want growth and recognition, then you have to be comfortable outside of your silo. Remember, there is no "I" in TEAM and you also have to realize that your team today goes far beyond your own department.

Question 13. What Is Your Best Form of Research?

Listening. Over the course of your career, you'll do a great deal of communicating, both written and spoken, offline and online too. But, regardless of the form of communication, you always have to listen first. Listening leads to truly understanding your audience needs. The information gained from listening can be used in different ways. For instance, feedback can be placed back into your product development cycle to make a better product, or information you uncover internally can educate management on how to better manage employees for smoother processes and operations. Listening helps you to personalize or customize customer communication, and it can also lead to more innovative pitches with the media.

Sometimes, when you are too close to the situation, you cannot "see the forest for the trees." You either have to step back and do some more listening, or get an outside perspective to shed some additional light for you. The bottom line is that listening will always be an important form of research and should continue throughout the duration of your communication programs (and your entire career).

Michelle Bacharach, the founder and CEO of FINDMINE, shared how listening helped to launch her business. After seeing consumers ask about 600 million questions a day through search engines, she founded her startup company. FINDMINE helps retailers to customize a consumer's shopping experience. Michelle's research and listening to people online helped her to solve their wardrobe issues. She created a tech platform to offer retailers the opportunity to cross reference and pair together different articles of clothing that looked good together, based on consumer preferences. Understanding the customers, their needs, and making it personal are the best ways to build loyal fans and lasting bonds.[4]

Go ahead, put on your big listening ears and keep them on as your best form of investigation and understanding. Your organization and your customers will thank you. Your own professional and personal growth will be your reward.

Question 14. How Curious Should You be About Your Competition?

No matter how big or small your company, be curious about your competition and watch them closely. You have to monitor the competitive landscape. Take a good look at what your competitors are doing and saying; don't be "boxed in" by what they do or how they are positioning themselves. The goal is not to be like them. You want to stand out and apart from them. When it comes to being curious about the competition, it really means you want to be different.

A word of caution … there is always competition. Don't accept the boss, client, or teammate who says there is no competition and that "no one is like us." There will always be competitors on some level, but you will have to determine some of the differentiating factors. In all my years in marketing, I have always managed to find a competitor for comparison.

Here is my short list of questions to help you be more curious about your competition:

- What is your competitor's positioning and messaging?
- What is the perception of your competitors in the industry?
- Has there been recent positive or negative communication about them?

Figure 1.2 Curious About the Competition

- What are the media and influencers in the industry saying about the competition?
- Where and how often do they communicate?
- How are they represented visually?
- What is the competitor customer experience like? Do some "mystery shopping" by getting a demo of their services and speaking with their sales representatives. You can also ask people to do this for you.
- How are your competitors doing financially?

Be curious and know your competition. Keep your eyes on them. Then, absorb what you learn to build your own unique brand. Deep curiosity is the characteristic of not only an avid learner but also a strong leader. Being curious will also help you to know what you do better and to capitalize on your strengths.

Question 15. Is PR Best Suited for the Small Marketing Budget?

PR can be implemented on the tightest marketing budget, as long as the commitment to building a relationship exists. Remember, with PR, you're paying for the time it takes you to build awareness, credibility, and relationships for a company, service/product, or to change audience opinion and maintain/protect a reputation.

Thankfully, you can do this with the tremendous amount of research and data at your fingertips through media audits, sales data, website analytics, customer service, and social media analytics. As a result, your programs can be much more targeted, which translates into less time wasted and not as much money spent. Today, it can take you a fraction of the time to reach the right audience with the information they want and need from you.

Here is an example. Your media pitches can be extremely hard hitting and attention grabbing based on the information you capture and analyze, and the intelligence you glean. There is no excuse for not knowing who, when, where, why, and how to build a relationship, by sharing information that's newsworthy, timely, and, most of all, of interest to your recipient and the members of their media community.

When Kingsford Charcoal wanted to call attention to coal at Christmas (for reasons other than black coal in your stocking), they found the right partner and worked efficiently and quickly to make some noise. They teamed up with Sysomos, the social media intelligence and data analytics company, to find the nicest person on social media. Sysomos analyzed over 100 billion tweets to learn that Clifford Brown, a resident of Waukesha, Wisconsin, was the nicest person on social media because he:

1. didn't use profanity in his tweets;
2. used words like "please" and "thank you" the most on Twitter;
3. was an avid griller, even in the wintertime.

Because Mr. Brown was immediately placed at the top of Santa's "nice" list, Kingsford awarded him a year's worth of coal, a Kingsford Kettle Grill and some grilling essentials. By using Twitter data to find the nicest person on social media, the story landed in a number of publications, from online grilling to social media publications, raising the awareness of charcoal and grilling at Christmastime.[5]

So, get your team ready for some data sharing and brainstorming (with your partners too). Pitch the newsworthy information that's at your fingertips. Your programs can be small and targeted, yet really effective, when PR is implemented on a shoestring budget.

Question 16. Do You Need a Straight or a Dotted Line to the C-Level?

Your best opportunity as a communicator occurs when you have direct access to the CEO or the senior-level executives in your company. Of course, being in this position takes a tremendous amount of trust. You're not only privy to sensitive business information and company growth strategies, but you are also relied upon to make important company announcements and to represent your organization.

Unfortunately, if you don't speak directly to the executives, and other professionals are communicating for you, then "layers of interference" may get in the way. In this case, the communication moving through layers can be diluted or weakened and you clearly won't have the executive insights and face-time you need. Plus, having a straight or dotted line to C-Level secures your seat at the boardroom table. Your relationship with executives should be a part of your career growth strategy.

Earlier in my career, I worked in a New York City branch of a PR agency. There were financial publications lying around the office, from the *Wall Street Journal* and *Barron's* to *Investor's Daily*. I would take a publication and read it at lunch and also take one home on the bus, making the commute time pass by a little more quickly. I made a point of asking questions about what I read to make sure I understood how some of the information related to our financial clients. I would also cross my name off of the small printed sheet at the top of these publications (they were inter-office reading materials) and always hand deliver a financial publication to the next executive on the list. I wanted to make sure he knew I was keeping up on my financial reading. Could I have handed it to a manager on the list? Sure, but I knew better.

My interest in the financial side of the agency's business and my constant curiosity allowed me to create that dotted line to a senior executive in the office. Why did he take an interest in me? Because I took an interest well beyond what was expected of my role, which helped me to get recognized much more quickly. Whether you're a young professional looking to be noticed or you're a little more seasoned, always take the time to further your interest and create that straight or dotted line.

Question 17. How Can You Make the CFO Your Best Friend Forever (BFF)?

If you want to get the CFO's attention, then think like one. Better yet, if you want to make a Best Friend Forever (BFF), then demonstrate how what you do every day delivers valuable outcomes. Share the business side of your communication results. Let your

CFO know that your focus is not on the clicks, likes, views, hits, and impressions. You are much more than HITS, describes Katie Paine, who says that's "How Idiots Track Success."[6]

Of course, sharing the volume of your stories and media coverage is part of the equation, but you must also make sure you can clearly show how these stories drive traffic to the company's website, and how people behave from there. These are the "trackable" outcomes favored by senior leadership. You want to uncover how people behave on your website or what actions they take on a specifically designed landing page in your campaign. Then, from click to conversation, you can demonstrate lead generation, which is very close to the CFO's heart.

Other outcomes appreciated by your CFO include how your work helps with brand health by averting negative issues and fostering positive public opinion, how the art of storytelling optimizes a marketing program, and how your communication helps to produce happy and more satisfied customers.

One of my best, and early, examples as a younger professional was a news story about an architectural client that I placed on the front page of a north Jersey publication. The story led to my client receiving calls about the design of a new school building. Several months later, they were signing a contract. One front page story turned into a lucrative project. We scored major points with the CFO and all the executives at the company.

Your CFO also wants news stories to reflect the growth of the business and to attract the interest of the business media. If you can achieve these activities and outcomes, then you'll have a BFF at your company in the form of a C-level friend.

Question 18. Will PR Ever be Your Sales Pitch?

Although PR and marketing work closely together and the lines continue to blur, there are still distinct differences. PR is considered the softest "selling" approach, unlike advertising, promotion, and direct selling. Yet, it is considered highly credible in the eyes of consumers. For this reason, your PR should not come across as sales or what's referred to as "marketing-speak." If your PR does cross the line, then you will hear about it quickly.

For example, every time you write a byline article for a publication, share a blog post, give a television interview, or commit to a speaking engagement, you would not use these opportunities as a direct sales pitch or an infomercial for yourself or your company. In fact, these forums require your thought leadership and sharing of your expertise and advice. However, you can use these types of platforms to be positioned as the expert, which, in turn, results in clients/customers and other stakeholders inquiring about your business.

In PR, the credibility you build through thought leadership will eventually become an instant gateway to getting the big "sale." PR implemented correctly means you can help to generate sales without ever having to cross the line into the really "salesy" territory.

Question 19. How Do You Become a Trusted Change Agent?

Believing in change, rallying for support, and implementing a transformation can be one of the scariest, yet rewarding experiences you can have. When you're a change agent, you believe in yourself and you step out of your own comfort zone. Through new experiences, you can apply your leadership, knowledge, focus, and courage, to develop and implement what needs to get done.

Creating change is never easy, especially in an organization where infrastructure may be rooted in an older and, sometimes, more "traditional" framework. However, just thinking about change and creating change are two entirely different animals. If you're a change agent, then you really want to spark action, which starts with finding others who have a similar goal or vision. You need a coalition, small or large, that will communicate the urgency to help make change happen.

At the same time, the change agent knows that communication about the change is paramount. If you can educate and guide others, then participation around the change will increase. Growing your army of change agents, who will rally for the change, will also be instrumental in the endorsements and small "wins" that you share. When these small winning moments occur, others may take notice and join your cause. You'll also see the naysayers slowly fade away.

Back in 2007, I started writing about the concept of PR 2.0 and the hybrid PR approach on my blog. For me, PR was becoming more integrated with marketing, and I noted how the practice of PR was changing as a result of social media. I received a lot of pushback from PR peers and colleagues. By 2008, when I attended the PRSA International Conference in San Diego, I had educators on the university level approach me about my views. Many of my colleagues felt I was blurring the lines too much. However, I saw the bridge to marketing and I started breaking down the silos between marketing and PR earlier and was vocal about the changes in my book, *PR 2.0*.[7]

I never stopped believing in the tremendous opportunities resulting from the blurred lines. There was, and still is, incredible potential for communication professionals to do more as integrated teams work together. Today, we see this collaboration and innovation in full force. Change can be daunting and sometimes a slow process. Be ready to face resistance, which is a sign that people are taking notice. However, the change agent never stops believing in herself and moving toward the transformation end goal. Be the change agent and the role model. Others will naturally take your lead and follow.

Question 20. How Can You Prove to Executives Your Communication (PR) Is Tangible?

PR is the hardest of all of the marketing disciplines to "sell" because the tangible results may take months or sometimes years to produce. What's the immediate value of building relationships? The value is often realized over time. However, there are tangibles you can quickly point out. The easiest is media coverage, which now extends well beyond print to online and social media endorsements. Another easy tangible is benchmarking the traffic and the sources that drive visitors to your website as a result of your PR outreach programs. Also, added to the list is hearing and showcasing testimonials from happy customers, from your case studies to what people share about on Facebook and Twitter.

Customers will always let you know how they feel. What about solving issues that could tarnish your brand? When you address a potential issue bubbling up on your blog, and turn a negative situation into a positive learning experience, then you're saving time and money. This, too, is tangible PR.

But, don't stop there; continue to watch what actions your customers take as a result of your communication. You should focus on their actions and dive deeper into their behaviors. Here are some of the important action-based questions to ask:

1. What do people do on your website and where do they spend the most time?

2. On social media, what do they like to do with you and what do they like to do on your behalf?
3. What important messages do people share the most about your brand and how often do they share them?

If you begin to identify and showcase the different tangibles, then you will experience how good PR can "sell" itself.

Question 21. Should You Participate in Pro Bono Work?

Throughout my career, professionals have shared how increasingly difficult it has become for them to participate in pro bono work. Reasons include the economy being in a recession and their scarce resources. Unfortunately, there will always be excuses. However, when you take the time and resources to invest in pro bono, your work is an excellent way to help a non-profit organization or a company with limited resources. At the same time, you can gain attention for your work and your give-back culture through the media exposure you generate.

Participating in pro bono work also positions your company as altruistic and one that cares about the community. After all, pro bono work is not just reserved for a certain size or type of company. Giving back to the community is important for all companies and all their professionals. The rewards clearly outweigh any excuses that might hold you back. Plus, the companies that pursue pro bono receive experience in different areas that may help them to build additional business opportunities in the future.

When you want to pursue pro bono work, here are a few ways to make the most of your participation:

1. Look for mutually beneficial opportunities so it's a win–win for all parties involved.
2. Make sure you have the skills and competencies required to participate in the pro bono work.
3. Put the terms of the pro bono work in writing so everyone is in agreement over the work and the deliverables.
4. Meet beforehand and talk often before accepting and beginning your pro bono work.

New experiences and giving back through pro bono work can make a difference and outweigh any of the excuses.

Question 22. How Do Creative People Help You to Increase Your Creative Quotient (CQ)?

In any profession, surround yourself with brilliant, creative people and you will thrive in your career. Regardless of your role, you can't afford to stop exercising your creative muscles. By surrounding yourself with very talented, artsy people, you will continue to learn, grow, and advance your own skills. Some of my favorite years in PR and marketing have been working with the designers at my former marketing communications agency. I would like to believe that some of their creative genius rubbed off on me.

As a rule, interact with the professionals who will motivate you to a higher creative plateau, whether they work with you directly or you're engaging with them remotely in your communities. Three ways I have taken advantage of creativity outside of my PR and marketing role include:

- attending social Meetups focused on the type of creativity you would only find outside of your own professional position and skillset. For example, Meetups with artists, designers, and tech visionaries really opened up my frame of reference;
- taking a group tour of an art museum and participating in the discussion with your group can be a deeper learning experience than just walking around the museum on your own;
- having your own dinner party or even a company get together will stimulate great conversation and creativity. But, be sure to invite guests who are from different cultures, careers, and geographies.

If you take advantage of new creative learning experiences by tapping into the knowledge and gifts of your artistic peers, then you will see your own Creative Quotient (CQ) rise.

Question 23. Why Should You Get More Intimate with Your Customers?

When you know your customers, it shows in your communication and in their actions. They engage with you on a deeper level and praise you for a more rewarding experience. Studying customer behavior will help you to understand their motivations, perceptions,

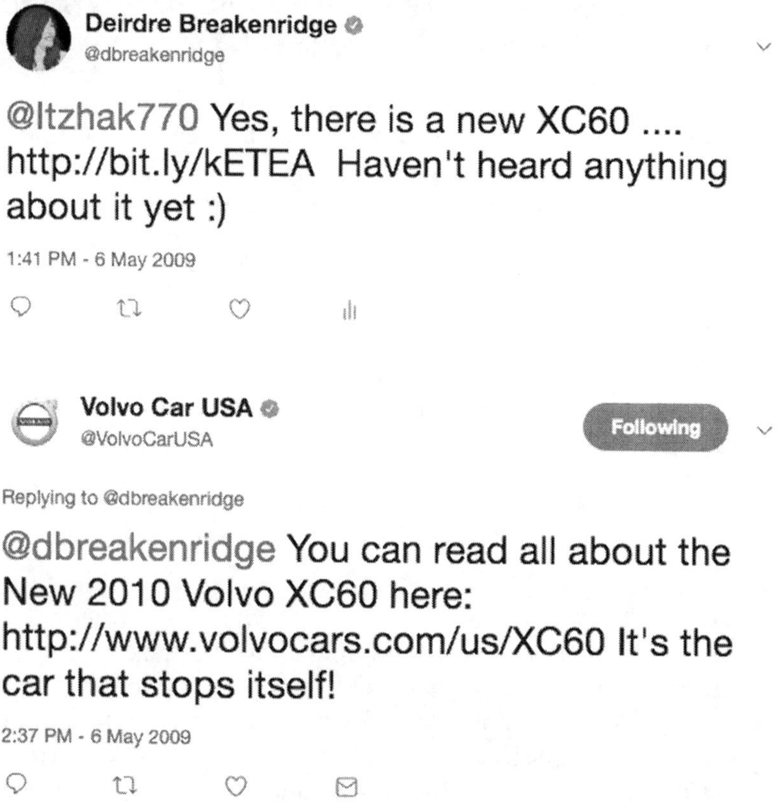

Figure 1.3 Brands Listening and Helping
Adapted from Twitter

influences, opinions, and purchasing patterns. Primary research is a great way to dig into audience habits and needs. Different methods include focus groups, surveys, polls, one-on-one interviews, usability studies, and even situations that warrant researchers to be placed in the business setting with audiences to monitor their behavior. You are gathering information first hand.

At the same time, uncovering social media conversations and data intelligence about your company and industry will tell you how your audience feels and what they like, and don't like, about your business. You should be monitoring your company's keywords to uncover important discussions about your company or your industry. At all times, you have to be listening closely and then use the feedback to show customers how much you value what they say.

I remember having a conversation on Twitter about one of my favorite car brands … Volvo. I consider my family to be a Volvo family. There are three Volvos in the driveway as proof of loyalty. In a Twitter conversation, a friend and I were discussing the Volvo XC60. I was shopping for a new car. I shared how I didn't know much about the XC60. Within a couple of minutes of my comment, @VolvoCarUSA jumped into our conversation, offering me more information on this new model, with a link to find out additional information. They also offered to answer any of my questions about the model I mentioned or any other model that might be of interest. This is the perfect example of a brand listening and being there to help me out in the decision-making process.

Being intimate with customers is an investment in them; your research, online and offline, when used wisely in your communication, shows your customers that you truly care.

Question 24. Why Do You Need a Contingency Plan for Every Situation?

This is an easy answer. Always have a contingency plan set in place. You may be thinking that the back-up plan only applies to a few scenarios. Think again. It's Murphy's Law that whatever can go wrong will, at any time. It didn't take me very long to realize that the concept of the contingency plan was critical to the success of my communication activities.

Here's why … your media tours will start later than expected; you will encounter Town Hall meetings with really tough questions for your executives; partners will face deadline issues affecting your campaign activities and timelines; planes will be delayed right before important events; and your team members have personal lives and their own problems. They get sick too. There are so many more scenarios that could negatively affect weeks of planning. During these situations, your contingency plan would have to be ready to kick into action.

When my agency was working with a client at a large media event in Las Vegas, I learned the value of a Plan "B". It was the day before our news media event at the National Association of Broadcasters (NAB). My Vice President (VP) was too ill to travel on a plane. I was left to handle all media activities at the booth and the press event … alone! Through excellent relationships I had forged with members of the client's product and marketing teams, I was able to enlist some additional help and delegate work to others that would have required me to be in two places at once. At the same time, I shifted members of my company who were on our client's advertising team, and also attending the conference, to the PR side. They, too, jumped in to assist with the event.

To this day, I'm ready for any scenario. My motto: If not Plan "A" then move to Plan "B." And, if you are really ambitious, then you'll have a Plan "C" in your back pocket as well.

Question 25. Is Your Communication Planned or Spontaneous Spaghetti Thrown Against the Wall?

The popular phrase, "throw it up and see where it sticks" is definitely not a phrase well-liked or embraced by communication professionals. Personally, I think it causes unnecessary anxiety. In this respect, I know I'm not alone. There's too much at stake for a company or an executive's reputation to leave anything to chance. For those of you who like to fly by the seat of your pants, you'll find that your company's communication is a serious business and only the strong, focused, and steady will survive. From day one, you have to be proactive and plan ahead, using research and intelligence to build a solid strategy; the exact opposite of the "throwing-the- spaghetti-on-the-wall" approach.

Planning and research should be at the heart of your communications. The effort you put into your marketing communication plan shows in your program results. Take the time to plan appropriately by figuring out your communication goals and objectives and appropriate messaging for target audiences. You will need to uncover the right channels to reach your audiences and build in a measurement program with benchmarks to prove that you're successful. Most of all, make sure everything you plan can be implemented because you have the resources—time, budget, and the people—to see the plan all the way through its execution.

If, by chance, you find that you only have some spaghetti on the wall, then please peel it off and start over with research and planning.

Question 26. Do You Really Need to be Ten Steps Ahead?

As a modern communicator, you need to be ready for the unexpected. But, how do you plan properly? You can be ready by constantly monitoring the business landscape and industry climate. Your job is to keep on top of the pulse of the marketplace and what economic, social, cultural, political and technological factors affect your company and your stakeholders related to these areas. By monitoring and understanding these areas and the constant changes, this will keep you abreast of the overall state of the industry.

Other ways to be ten steps ahead include understanding and articulating market size and growth, the scope of the competition, the level of product or service differentiation, and the rate of potential profitability.

At the same time, it's important to understand any hostile environments and threatening moves by competitors. If you can constantly access and keep this information current, you're much better prepared to handle any communication situation that may arise. At the same time, you'll also be able to hang out at the boardroom table and engage in more than just small talk with the C-Level executives.

Understanding the business of communication, going far beyond the planning of your pitches and media outreach, really helped me (and my clients) to always be ten steps ahead.

Question 27. Can Good Communications Solve All Your Company's Problems?

You may be incredibly organized and connected to the best media contacts or partners in your industry. Perhaps you're extremely proficient at what you do and it shows in your work. But, great communication can only go so far. If your company does not live up to the standards you're setting, then the result of your efforts will be useless. You can't say one thing and then do another. In the end, your hard work may end up highlighting all the negative behavior surrounding your organization, rather than accentuating the very positive information you set out to share.

Regardless of your ability to build relationships with different groups, secure great interviews with major media outlets, or motivate people inside your company and external audiences too, your company has to make sure it delivers on all of its promises. People who believe in your brand promise will evaluate you on whether they have a great experience each and every time they interact with you.

Excellent PR and great communication will not cover up a lousy product, crummy customer service, bad employee behavior, or deceitful practices. You have to fix what is broken, starting on the inside first. Then, when you're back on the right track, you can use PR to accentuate the positive and highlight what really stands out about your company.

Question 28. Why Should You be Patient and Never Lose Your Cool?

If you're a modern communicator, then you may work with anxious customers, annoyed executives, frustrated employees, and short-tempered journalists. Situations can be tense; it's the nature of any fast-paced business. However, if you lose your patience your attitude is a direct reflection of your company; the people that you represent or your own personal brand. Losing your temper once can immediately send red flags to the party who is on the receiving line.

Unfortunately, people remember great communication less often and are quick to point out what they don't like and their less-than-pleasant interactions. Depending upon the situation, it's best to thoroughly hear the complaint, nasty comment, or unpleasant remark. Step back, count to ten, breathe, and formulate a response that is not based on your own personal emotions. Try to remove yourself from the situation. You need to become an observer of your own self. Then, coming back with a clear head will certainly help.

When I was feeling out a story with a media outlet, I came across a journalist who was very unhappy with my pitch angle. Back in the days of extensive pitching by telephone, after I delivered the quick story idea, the journalist snapped at me. He called me uninformed, and a "not well-read PR person." He also told me that I wasted his time. I was shocked at his reaction, especially when our client and my internal team had come up with the angle together. We had all read numerous issues of the magazine and did our homework extensively on the journalist and his publication.

Being a young and sensitive professional, I really wanted to fire back, just to let this cranky journalist know we worked really hard on this story. However, a *big* voice inside told me to *wait, breathe* and just *listen*. I kept my cool and told him that I would take his comments back to my team and that I appreciated his candor. Well, he didn't know what to do with my very nice and sincere response. Quickly gaining his composure, he told me he was having a bad day. After the call, we ended up tweaking the angle for this journalist to fit into a piece he was already working on for his magazine. And, so the story goes, it was a win–win for all involved.

What I learned through the experience ... be patient, because losing your cool may frustrate you more, and will not solve any of the issues at hand. Plus, you definitely get more bees with honey.

Question 29. Why Should You Create a Strategy and Then Implement Your Tactics?

If you don't take the time to create a strategy, then don't bother with your communication tactics. The strategy part is your roadmap or your approach. Your strategy is knowing your goals and objectives (specifically what you want to achieve), understanding your audience because you have done your research, and identifying how you will reach them with different messaging through the appropriate channels. When you have a strategy in place, you also set your measurement benchmarks and the budget that will be required.

Developing a communication program takes time. You don't want to rush the strategy and planning part or skimp on your research. Your research helps you to fully understand your audience and the situation. Some companies formulate their plans every six months and some construct their plans more frequently. And, now with social media, planning can actually be done in real time because of the instantaneous feedback loop from your customers and other stakeholders. Regardless of the timing, strategy always comes first.

At the same time, every part of your roadmap has to be realistic, with the right resources in place. A good plan, with a solid strategy, lets you roll out and easily manage your communication tools and tactics, which may include your news releases, blog articles, emails, social media posts, etc., through different channels. If your strategy is really good, then you'll be measuring significant outcomes as a result of the activities you put into place.

For your program's success ... always think strategy first and then communication tactics. Also, because you're in real time, remember to evaluate often and make adjustments as needed.

Question 30. What Is the Best Way to Brainstorm?

Brainstorming is a great way to open up a wider canvas of creative ideas. In my experience, the best brainstorming teams are made up of individuals in marketing/PR, as well as those outside of your own department. When creating the brainstorming team, you should select people in your company who are uninhibited, unbiased, and can step outside of their comfort zones. These individuals should be among the team members who do not have "preconceived" notions or feel restrained by any prior marketing knowledge.

When you set up your winning brainstorm team, you can also set a few parameters in place for a more creative session, including:

1. making people feel it is okay to share their "far out ideas";
2. helping teammates to feel comfortable about articulating what they like and what they don't like about an idea (always sharing why they don't think an idea will work);
3. playing the devil's advocate approach to every idea—to hear the pros and cons;
4. demonstrating how to build on a concept, sharing different approaches and options.

At all times, try to get away from the usual boardroom setting for these meetings. Take the team into a different and more relaxed area of the company or go offsite altogether to get the creative juices flowing. If you only incorporate typical brainstorming into your process, then you will only generate typical ideas.

Question 31. Is It Important to Take a Proactive Approach for Yourself?

Being proactive really counts for your company and for you too. Many of the larger brands, such as Coke, Pepsi, Wal-Mart, Google, Apple, etc., clearly have a media edge. Their reputation and size in their industries afford these companies the steady media coverage they receive. The media knocks on their doors for information constantly. They are always in the news, with the feel-good stories and sometimes the negative coverage too. If you are not the "media darling" in your industry, then you have to think of creative ways to get in front of the media.

Remember, the media need executives who can provide valuable insight on hot topics and pressing issues. You should always be thinking about creative ways to tell your story, tied to what is going on in the news, affecting your industry, or even your local community. Opening up the PR opportunities to other areas of your company allows your internal subject-matter experts (SMEs) to share a different perspective or something unique that you may not even know. You can also try sharing some fresh statistics with the media about your market or your customers using creative visuals or in a more interactive way. Lastly, you can talk to different departments in your company to find out what they are doing differently, and what is new and interesting in their work.

You would be surprised at the variety of topics and stories that result from being proactive and from asking different questions from untapped sources that are right within your own four walls.

Question 32. How Do You Identify Your Partners and Create Opportunities Together?

You can't be all things to all people. Working with partners, skilled in areas that you're not, will allow you to focus on what you do best. The most rewarding relationships exist when there is a clear delineation of responsibilities and functions. Partners are complementary to your service offerings. Finding these partners will open up your business and products to their networks and vice versa.

As a small marketing communication agency of about 40+ people, we had realized that we could not be everything to everyone. It was a hard lesson for entrepreneurs who wanted to do *so* much to serve our clients. We tried to build everything in-house, which was an expensive proposition. We hired a pool of copywriters, increased our design staff, and even began hiring programmers to build out our web development capabilities. What we learned quickly ... the best resources are highly paid and you don't want to skimp on your clients' work. At the same time, hiring people meant an incredible amount of overhead, from the square footage of the workspace to the workplace insurance for all these new employees.

As time went on and there was more acceptance about the remote work teams, we realized that we didn't need to have everyone be onsite. We also didn't need an employee to fill every single marketing role. In great partners, we found excellent copywriting services, web designers, and programmers (beyond just a core few). We didn't need big departments filled with creative people, but we did need big pools of creative people who we could trust. Relying on industry friends and associations and our ability to constantly network, we built up a strong partner base.

Of course, every partner has to be a trusted resource. You must do your homework and screen your partners carefully. A partner is an extension of your brand and one that has, at times, access to your customers and employees. When you're aligning your brand, always be sure your brand is in very good company.

Question 33. What Is the Best Way to Exercise Your Creative PR?

Creative PR is matching your creative and interactive storytelling with the messages you need to communicate, while being able to measure your great results. The right side of the brain meets left side; creativity unites with analytical thinking. The key is to always be creative with purpose.

You may have the responsibility of maintaining and protecting your brand's public reputation or maybe even the company stock price. However, this does not mean you cannot stretch the imagination to make your communication more passionate, human, and attention-getting for all the right reasons.

I remember working with a regional medical center in Florida. They really needed a creative way to increase awareness nationally about their hospital community—from their physicians and administrators to their staff. They creatively raised the bar by sharing more human and intimate details about the key physicians at the hospital. Doctors are real people too. They employed world-renowned doctors on staff, but they were also just as human as the guy or gal next door.

Videos on the site showed the doctors in action … from doing their rounds and surgical procedures to discussing very complicated procedures. At the same time on the hospital's website were videos of these same doctors doing what they loved in their free time. One doctor was playing the guitar and singing along to his own handwritten music. Reaching into the depth of their own people and sharing something different definitely raised this hospital's creativity bar.

Here is a good rule to follow … your communication, regardless of the industry, does not have to translate into mundane, routine, or even boring information. Creative PR lets you deliver communication that's more interesting, visually pleasing, and highly informative and meaningful. But, most of all you should be able to show how your creativity impacts and grows your business.

Question 34. What Do You Do When a Situation Looks Grim?

You may be faced with some tough situations that need to be handled delicately. Even when things get rough, you should keep a positive attitude as you push forward to solve the challenge or problem and neutralize negative issues. Research says our brains are wired to be in survival mode and often project the worst possible scenarios. Yes, it's true, as a modern communicator you may have to think of all of the worst-case scenarios and how they may play out.

However, there are more reasons for you to remain positive both for productivity and your own health benefits, as well as for those around you. As a matter of fact, studies show that being negative or pessimistic can lead to depression and other health issues. Staying positive and calm as a communicator, even when the situation looks grim, is not only a quicker path to a solution but also the key to helping others around you to keep their composure in a trying situation.

When the situation looks grim, here's what you can do:

1. Step back, take a deep breath and gather all the facts quickly.
2. Listen and hear from different sources to gain valuable perspective.
3. Don't fear communication, but use it as a way to be transparent and inform the people who matter.
4. Step outside of an emotional situation and be a clear-headed observer who can respond appropriately.
5. Use your words carefully and understand just who they'll impact, and how.
6. Never let them see you sweat. You can fall apart when the situation is back under control or headed in a better direction.

Dale Carnegie wrote a well-known book, *Stop Worrying and Start Living*.[8] When it comes to a situation that looks grim, do what Dale Carnegie says ... ask yourself what's the worst that can happen and then face that reality. In the end, it may not be as horrible as you think.

Question 35. What Is Better, Being an "A" or a "B"-type Personality in Communications?

Type "A" personalities are known for moving quickly and conquering tremendous tasks in a short amount of time. However, if you ever find yourself wrapped up in doing a lot and just going through the motions without a clear picture, then take a moment to step back. It may be time to incorporate some Type B perspective into your regimen.

Type B personalities are more likely to step back, think clearly, and connect the dots. When you remove yourself from your crazy cycle of busy communication tactics, you can visualize the big picture and strategically move toward your goals. Suddenly, you're able to connect the dots. As a communicator, it's the difference between being tactical in your approach and strategically planning for what you want to achieve and then moving toward the success of your program.

Avoid jumping from dot to dot, or randomly skipping from stone to stone. See how and why these dots strategically tie together and map your course with greater purpose and a clearer understanding of your situation. At times, you'll want to harness your "A" tendencies to get a lot done, but not before you've capitalized on being a "B" type by connecting the strategic dots.

Question 36. What Does It Mean to "Command a Presence" in the Room?

Don't just enter the room; you need to command the room. You can make your presence known by standing tall with great posture and with the tone of your voice, right down to the clothes that you're wearing. Now, this doesn't mean you have to run out and spend thousands of dollars on fancy outfits. But what it does mean is that you have to show you care; from how you communicate to your physical appearance and presence.

When you take the time to care about your presence, you come across as someone who is polished and interested in serious discussions. Even the strength of your handshake and how you make eye contact will let people know that you mean business. The way you come across with your first impression will help to determine:

1. if your information is well received; and
2. whether new doors will open, leading to more successful interactions and relationships.

Have you ever noticed how performers in a theater production enter onto the stage? They almost glide with grace and physical prominence. What about members of the military; how do they stand when they are in a formation? Even when they're "at ease," their stance is strong and ready.

Here is one of my favorite tips: When you enter a room, whether it's a meeting room or you're on stage for a presentation, it's important to keep your feet firmly planted about a foot or so apart, almost as if you are assuming a military stance. Then, as you speak, you open your arms wide in a welcoming fashion, drawing your audience right into your discussion.

Of course, these tips take time and practice. When you learn to command the room, everyone will know you have arrived!

Question 37. Can You "Control" Your Own People?

I've prepared executive speaking points for years, whether they were for company announcements, one-on-one interviews, or news conferences in a Q&A setting. Speaking points keep executives focused on the key messages. Prepared executives can work these messages into almost any interview response. However, no matter how many points are discussed and prepared prior to the delivery, a couple of situations can occur.

For example, your executive may appreciate having the points on hand. However, she doesn't take ample time to review them. Then, there's the executive who prefers to "shoot from the hip," which is the more preferred and natural speaking style, but could prove to be the worst-case scenario for you, the communication expert.

I remember preparing a high-profile athlete for a news conference at his annual charity event. The PR team felt very well prepared for any journalist's questions that came our client's way. Feeling very confident, it was time to make our way into the conference. Just as we were walking into the room where the media were waiting, I asked our client if he had any questions about the messaging points we had prepared. He stopped, looked me squarely in the eyes and said, "You mean what you sent me? Uh, thanks, but no ... I think I'll just wing this one."

Ugh. Not exactly what the PR team wants to hear. Let's just say this news conference was not the best one during the tenure of this athlete's professional career.

The Experts Weigh In

Sandra Fathi, President, Affect

Lead by Example

When I was 19, I volunteered for the Israeli Army. I was born in the U.S. and attended New York University my first year of college. When I decided to go abroad for my sophomore year, I chose Hebrew University of Jerusalem because I had some family in Israel and thought it would be an easy transition. I had a wonderful roommate from New Jersey who was a true Zionist (someone who believes in the Jewish nation) but more than her love for Israel, she had a keen understanding that all the cute guys our age were in the army. Essentially, every Israeli, men and women, serves in the Israeli army. Men serve for three years and women for two. We were clearly missing out. Together, we dropped out of school and volunteered to serve in the army.

My time in the Israeli military taught me about the true meaning of leadership. My experience was nothing like American movies about the army—with a sergeant or veteran officer standing on the side lines barking orders at soldiers to march, run or drop for 50 push-ups while he stared at a stop watch never breaking a sweat. In the Israeli army, your commanders are only about six months older—sometimes a year or two. They barely have a few minutes more experience than the soldiers they are leading. In addition, Israelis are known for being fiercely independent, feisty, and completely defiant when it comes to authority. There is no respect for rank or power in the military—soldiers talk back to commanders, they disobey orders, they don't fear military jail. So, how do you lead a group of soldiers in this environment? You lead by example. You lead by earning their trust. You lead by demonstrating that no one is willing to work harder, no one knows more about the mission, and no one cares about them more than you.

That is the only way to get soldiers to follow you into battle—and in Israel, with enemies surrounding the state, and a looming threat of war literally a few miles from their homes, the struggle is real. An Israeli commander is at the front of his squad, not at the back, the first to risk his or her life, the first to encounter danger, the first to take a bullet. You would never ask a soldier to do something that you as a commander would not do yourself. And they know it.

Although public relations never rises to the intensity of going to war, the same principles apply when it comes to leadership. For the past 14 years, I have run my own agency and I've never asked a team member to do anything that I wouldn't do myself. I am continuously learning new skills and acquiring new tools to improve my craft and impart that knowledge on my team members. I am unwavering when it comes to the quality of my work, and anything that leaves the walls of our agency. However, at the same time, my employees know that I have their backs—I won't ask them to sacrifice their principles for the sake of a paying client. I won't ask them to work 80-hour weeks because I believe they too should spend time with their families. I'll do what needs to be done to protect them, to provide them with the compensation, skills, and the tools they need to accomplish any mission, and I'll lead fearlessly into any battle.

Heather Whaling, President, Geben Communication

Partnering and Connecting Are Your Competitive Edge

Did you know there are PR agencies that offer "networking" as a paid service? Meaning, they'll open their contacts, facilitate introductions, and make meaningful connections—for a fee.

For some, that's a business model that works. For me, I've found that creating partnerships and making those connections isn't a service … it's my competitive edge.

How can that be? And, why would I willingly give away something that other people are monetizing?

A few years ago, we were working with a local government agency that was preparing to launch a new service. Young professionals who live and/or work in downtown Columbus were a key target demographic to reach. Our scope of work with this client was narrow—limited to social media community management. But, we had a very strong relationship with the local Yelp community manager and saw an opportunity for our client to partner with Yelp to reach this audience. So, we facilitated an introduction and scheduled a lunch meeting. From there, we stepped out, but the partnership that evolved turned into a win–win for both parties. That client renewed their contract with us and the Yelp community manager continues to be an excellent advocate for that client (and many of our other ones).

As communicators, it's our job to build trust and improve relationships (it is *public relations,* after all!). Instead of hoarding connections, open your network. Look for opportunities to make meaningful introductions or to facilitate mutually beneficial partnerships. That's how you build a strong network, with yourself in the middle. A mentor once told me that the person in the center of the network owns the network. Instead of viewing networking as a necessary evil, shift your perspective. Embrace it as your competitive advantage.

Karen Freberg, Assistant Professor at the University of Louisville and Adjunct Lead Instructor at West Virginia University's IMC Graduate Online Program

Train Like an Olympian

Being proactive and successful in the communications field does not happen overnight. I have this conversation many times with students coming in and out of my office or sending me a late-night tweet about what they need to do to be successful in the PR, social media, or communications field.

My short answer is: You have to embrace the mentality of an Olympian and train like one. As a former student athlete in track and field, I ended my athletic career as a four-time All-American in the shot put, University of Southern California shot put school record holder, two-time SEC champion, and a 2004 Olympic Trials finalist.

Working, teaching, and practicing in digital media taught me a lot of life lessons I still share with my students. To be successful in the PR and social media field is very similar to being a track and field athlete, such as:

You are expected to perform and be on your "A" game if you work in social media and PR: The field is changing so much, you have to make sure you have your hand on the pulse of the industry. Each pitch, meeting, performance, and presentation you make you have to be at your very best. Everyone will be looking at what you are doing while tweeting, snapping, and sharing your insights for the world to see.

Know how you compare to other athletes (professionals) out there in the industry: Like athletics, you want to make sure you are preparing the best you can for the upcoming competition. You always want to see what everyone else is up to and have a few cards up your sleeve to pull out at any given time. Do your research, see what other professionals in the industry are doing, and make sure you address your strengths and work on your weaknesses. You can learn something from everyone—educate yourself and see what you can do to bring something new and unique to the table.

Train like an Olympian with your work in PR and social media: I used to work out 7 to 8 hours a day back as a collegiate athlete. From weightlifting to throwing, I was trying to master my sport and event to the best of my ability. There were days where everything worked and you had the best possible conditions to compete and practice. Then, there are days where everything goes wrong and the last thing you want to do is pick yourself up after not performing well. How you react to failure defines how you will prepare to achieve success. The same can be said about working in social media. While I am no longer throwing things, I am still "training" in my work ethic in social media. You have to do a little bit each day and set time aside for studying, reading, and practicing your work like an athlete. There are days where you are on top of the world, and then there are days where you have to advise clients who are experiencing a crisis. You don't become an Olympian (or influencer/thought leader) overnight. It takes time, persistence, and dedication.

Every PR pro (or athlete) trains differently: Everyone has a different approach they like to take when it comes to educating (training) for their craft. You want to see what works best for you based on the way you approach the field even to deciding what times of the day work best for you to write, brainstorm ideas, and create content in social media.

Embrace your own brand as a pro (athlete): Never feel like you have to be like everyone else. You want to be your own person and make sure you are communicating this yourself. You are your best PR professional—no one else knows you better than you. Same thing as an Olympian, you never want to feel like you have to be like everyone else in your event (or industry). I wasn't the typical shot putter competing and I tell my students all the time I am approaching being a professor in a different way. Don't try to be like everyone else. Do what works for you. Showcase your personality and embrace your brand, and be the strongest advocate on why you are unique compared to others. You sometimes have to be your own best PR person.

Notes

1 PR Expanded, Kirk Hazlett article, "Ethics 'Month': Why Not Make it a Lifetime?", September 10, 2012. Available at: www.deirdrebreakenridge.com (accessed May 22, 2017).
2 PRSA.org Website, Definition of PR, About PR Section, 2012. Available at: http://apps.prsa.org/AboutPRSA/publicrelationsdefined/ (accessed May 22, 2017).
3 Women Worldwide Podcast, "Samantha Paxson Discusses Women in Tech & Financial Services," August 14, 2016.
4 Women Worldwide Podcast, "Michelle Bacharach Shares Insights on Startup Life and Retail Tech," August 28, 2016.
5 Yahoo! Finance, News Release, "The Nicest Person in Social Media," December 14, 2012.
6 Steve Goldstein, PR News, "Katie Paine's 5 Data Points You Need in Your PR Dashboard," October 22, 2015. Available at: www.prnewsonline.com/water-cooler/2015/10/02/5-data-points-you-need-in-your-pr-dashboard/ (accessed May 22, 2017).
7 Deirdre Breakenridge, *PR 2.0, New Media, New Tools, New Audiences* (New York: FT Press, A Pearson Education Company, April 2008).
8 Dale Carnegie, *How to Stop Worrying and Start Living* (New York: Gallery Books, October 2004).

Chapter 2

Growing Relationships Built to Last

What is the secret to growing relationships that are built to last? Time, effort, focus, and knowing what you put into a relationship will show in the strength of the connection over time. Remember, creating connections, and growing them, is more about the people you meet and less about finding your own opportunity. There is no secret potion or easy checklist to guarantee that a relationship will last a lifetime, a year, or even for an intense moment.

At times, you may see relationships quickly surface in your career and then go away just as fast. However, when you can get to the heart of what people need and you deliver consistently as a reliable, trustworthy, and attentive "friend," then your relationships will develop to a higher level and for a longer time. For me, every relationship is unique. But, the relationships that are built to last start with a deep understanding around your connection. Then, they build upon the enthusiasm and great *mutual* synergy, which continues over time. Now, you may think it is easy to start a relationship, and in most cases, you may be right. But it is how you nurture and develop the connection over time that makes the difference.

Friendships can spark anywhere and anytime. How you approach the relationship matters the most, regardless of where you meet. I have met some of my best friends through the physical work environment. When you work with people eight plus hours a day, you become a family and deep friendships form. At the same time, some of my other best friends I have met through professional associations and interactions that began on Twitter, long before I ever met them in person. The old excuse of "they live so far away" or "we really don't get to spend time together" doesn't work in an age of social conversations and technology that allows you to cross borders and boundaries with your communication. The principles you apply in your personal relationships are the same professionally.

The success of your relationships has more to do with your mindset than your physical proximity.

In this chapter, the questions and answers presented will help you to take steps from simple connections that begin with casual conversations down a long and winding path to form stronger, longer-term bonds. At the same time, you'll also learn the art of connecting your most valued contacts in your network and helping them to build successful relationships that are also built to last.

Question 38. Is Wasting Someone's Time the Anti-relationship Builder?

If you are trying to build a relationship, then you want to be very respectful of someone's time. For example, if you book an appointment in person, by telephone, or by video call then you should not only show up on time but also be ready to engage in meaningful discussion. The translation: You are enthusiastic and serious about the potential of the relationship right from the start.

Of course, we all know "life happens," and there are times when meetings are missed or even rescheduled at the last minute. A note of caution … when you're dealing with busy professionals, sometimes you don't get a second chance for a first meeting, or a first impression. Keeping your appointments, and showing up eager and prepared, says a lot about you and how you want a relationship to move forward.

I remember a young professional who asked me to chat with him about his career goals. He wanted to pick my brain, as he was transitioning into an important new role at his company. I was happy to set up a call to mentor him. However, when the time came, he didn't reach out as planned. Instead, he emailed later that day to explain something had come up and he was unable to make our call. We ended up rescheduling for another day, which unfortunately came and went. Once again, I heard nothing from him at our scheduled time. Like the first incident, there was another excuse. He said, "Duty called … I had to jump into something," claiming there was no way for him to reach out.

How do you think this story ended? Was a third call scheduled? At that point, we had hit an unfortunate roadblock, and the relationship suffered. Relationships flourish when both parties are fully invested and they honor the agreed-upon time commitment.

Question 39. How Does Saying "No" Help Your Relationships?

You may find yourself busy building a number of critical relationships. However, this should never reach the point of aggravation, pressure, or fatigue. There will always be a plethora of events, social gatherings, and online discussions that will interest you. Yes, the Internet never sleeps and neither does social media. However, you do. Know when to decline an invitation gracefully by saying "No." You only have so many hours in a day and the choices you make will help you to stay happy and healthy. Working too much, and finding you're over-extended is not good, personally or professionally. As a result, all your relationships will suffer.

When my daughter, Megan, was eight years old, I was a solo mom. She taught me how to say "No." At the time, I was an agency owner and author. I remember one of our mommy–daughter interactions after I wrote my second book, *The New PR Toolkit*.[1] As an author, I found myself getting increasingly busy between work, networking, taking interviews on off-hours (to accommodate the media), and additional speaking engagements to discuss my book. From my daughter, I learned that the gift of time should never be taken for granted.

One day, we were sitting on the floor playing a game and she said, "Mommy are you paying attention to me?" She knew I wasn't. My mind was clogged with book- and work-related obligations. I was physically there, sitting on the floor, but not mentally. Her sad voice and disappointment spoke volumes to me. I knew what I had to do. I decided to slow it down and be more selective with my activities. From that day onward, our time together became more fun, focused, and meaningful. It became easier to say "No" to average opportunities, knowing someday my daughter would not want to sit on the floor with me any longer. Learning to say "No" was the best decision I've ever made for our relationship. To this day (she's 22 as of the date of this writing), we may not be sitting on the floor playing games, but we are still best friends.

By taking the time to refocus your energy and not spreading yourself too thin, you'll find renewed meaning in your relationships and you'll be much more productive. When you start saying "No" to every opportunity, you begin to carefully select the best opportunities, becoming a much more present participant in your interactions with family, friends, and at work too.

Saying "No" helps you to pursue the best connections, and to also focus on growing the right relationships.

Question 40. How Do You Balance Tech with the Human Side of Relationships?

There are plenty of tools, platforms, and online communities to connect you with anyone you want to reach. You have many choices, from discussion forums and online groups to social networking and community discussions, to find your new connections. Perhaps, you're linking publically or privately through LinkedIn, Twitter, or Facebook. Technology serves one very important purpose: to facilitate better human interactions. But, remember, it's the human, in-person contact that is still, by far, the most valuable of your interactions.

Your goal should be to move from the virtual into the physical realm, being transparent and human every step of the way. I would choose an in-person meeting over any type of virtual meeting. Remember, when you're online you can't shake a hand, pat someone on the back, or give a friendly hug hello. Using an emoticon or an emoji is not the same thing. Although it's pretty cool to design your own personal bitmoji (I have one that looks and dresses like me). Still, it's not the same!

Early on, I admit, I was skeptical of online relationships. However, I experienced the ultimate in relationship building that started in the virtual world and then moved to IRL (In Real Life). I don't remember what year @Fogfish and I started tweeting back and forth. Our conversation started as a casual "hello" that went on for weeks. From that point, we moved to direct message (DM) and chatted back and forth, sharing resources, ideas, and building a friendship. It wasn't until about three years after we began our Twitter friendship that I finally met my friend in San Francisco, when I was speaking at the PRSA International Conference. I felt like we knew each other for so much longer.

Our back and forth via DM formed a solid friendship over the years. Right after this very meeting, we worked on a project together. He was kind enough to design my PR Hybrid Honeycomb infographic, to visually represent my eight new PR practices from my book, *Social Media and Public Relations*.[2] With the help of my husband, we built a website where people could download the poster and the different PR roles related to their careers. I'm still direct messaging him to this very day. Real relationships can start online.

Of course, if you can't be in the same room then utilizing technology to simulate being in person is the next best thing. Every opportunity to meet virtually gets you one step closer to the most human type of interaction you can have.

Question 41. Why Can't Everyone be a Best Friend Forever (BFF)?

One important lesson to learn early, both on the personal and professional front, is that not everyone will be a part of your inner circle of trust. Only those people you consider your confidants will be there to help and support you. Understand there are contacts who are your closest friends and colleagues. They will add value to your work or life, vs those who may participate with you on a very different level.

For instance, you may have contacts you visit when you're traveling to different cities, and there are also those who you only chat with on Twitter, Facebook, or LinkedIn. The latter contacts are still very important and you can certainly find great value in those relationships as they grow in time. They may be sharing interesting insights and you're bonding through your social media channels. Perhaps, with these contacts, your relationship is based on knowledge sharing and learning together in an online environment. These relationships should not be overlooked.

For example, I'm actively involved in Twitter communities, including #PRStudChat and #WinnieSun chat, and I also love participating in #MeasurePR. Participating in Twitter chats is a great opportunity to cultivate relationships with your online friends. Not every new contact will be a BFF, but the learning opportunity is invaluable. For your online friends, there are simple steps you can take, for example, after a Twitter chat to keep the relationship learning and growing:

1. Follow those who share the most interesting insights during the Twitter chat session and continue the discussion by reaching out with questions or additional relevant information.
2. Find your new contacts in other networks where they may be participating. Are they also on LinkedIn, Instagram, Facebook, and do they blog regularly? Get to know your new friends better by seeing what else they do and by checking out where else they participate.
3. Write a blog post about the chat session and the community's participation. You can use Storify, which is a useful tool to capture the best tweets of the discussion. Be the champion who shares the entire story and let your new friends know that they are included in your recap.

4. If the Twitter chat hashtag is popular, and used frequently post discussion, follow along on a daily basis to engage more frequently with the people you met during the Twitter chat discussion.

You will learn to identify different types of relationships over the course of your career. It's a give and take. You can't be all things to all people. But, if you can understand the dynamics of each relationship and the mutual benefits, then this will help you to invest the right amount of time and effort, from your BFFs to your more casual online acquaintances.

Question 42. How Do You Become a CRA (Chief Relationship Agent)?

Modern communicators are skilled relationship builders. They know the best relationships take time to cultivate and are based on trust. Think about your relationships at work, school, family, and with your friends. What do those relationships mean to you? Do you work at them every day? Do you give them your steady focus? Do you go the distance to protect these relationships because they are so important to you?

As you continue to develop and nurture your own relationships, part of becoming a CRA is knowing the value of your relationships and always keeping your contacts sacred. You should only share them with the utmost care. As a part of any good relationship, people trust you with their business information, their successes and challenges, and their time. So, if you decide to make an introduction on behalf of a contact with someone else in your network, then you must truly believe there will be synergy between the professionals you unite. When I make introductions, the goal is for my contacts to benefit and grow together as a result. By continuing down this connection path, your friends, colleagues, and peers will appreciate you as someone who has moved from relationship builder to what is called relationship "agent" status and trusted resource.

I have always said my career goes far beyond just relationship building. As a Chief Relationship Agent (CRA), my goal is to make the connections where other people thrive and excel together. The greatest satisfaction is seeing the fruits of someone else's labor and knowing you were instrumental in their successful outcome. But, it all starts with the importance you place on your relationships and what those relationships mean to you.

Question 43. How Can Your "Marketing Family" Create Experiences Together?

Marketing is a big family with all different professionals who share a common goal ... the growth and well-being of the brand. Thankfully, the silos are breaking down and PR is very much integrated with marketing. This is nothing new; I've always viewed PR as a big part of the marketing world for a few reasons:

Reason 1: Communication must be consistent, from brand messaging and imagery to every consumer experience at various touch points.

Reason 2: You need a mix of media to capture the attention of the highly-connected consumer in a noisy media landscape. Marketing is not enough and neither is PR. Today a combination of targeted messages, customized content, and meaningful ways to engage with audiences (where and when they want to connect with you) will get their attention and allow you to keep it.

Reason 3: No one area can do it alone and you don't want to cannibalize your own efforts. I've seen companies do this just by not connecting the entire communication team internally.

Reason 4: It takes an army of champions to maintain and protect brand reputation. PR has led the charge and sets a great example, but more champions from every area of the company need to join the reputation task force.

I remember working with a non-profit organization focused on consumer healthcare. When I first started working with the group I conducted a quick audit of their brand through various communication channels. I shared with the internal communications team how one part of the marketing organization was not sharing crucial information to support other areas, including public relations. For example, if you took a cross section of their social media profiles, from Twitter and Facebook to their YouTube channels, you would have seen different imagery, logos, messages, and an inconsistent

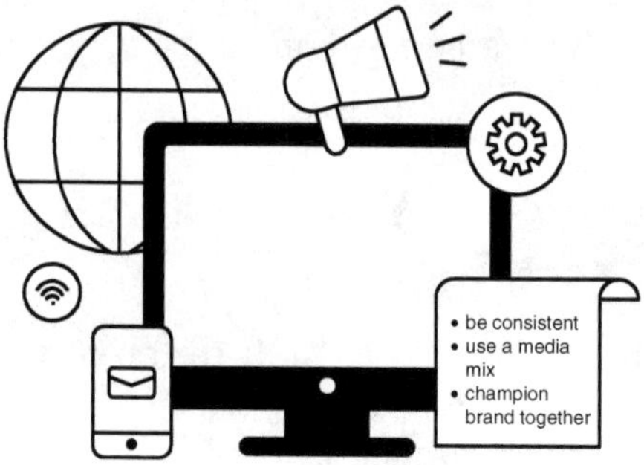

Figure 2.1 Reasons Why PR and Marketing Work Together

brand. They quickly worked to rectify the situation. Their solution was to halt any further disjointed appearance and messaging from occurring by building a better internal communication system. Everyone had to be on the same page and working to support one another.

PR builds brand awareness, credibility, trust, thought leadership, and relationships; marketing reinforces messages and—through visual, interactive, and compelling content—helps to drive engagement, leads, and sales, or—in the case of a non-profit organization—membership. Together, PR and marketing create the communication to build loyalty and brand advocacy. The two are greater than the sum of their parts. You have to know the PR and marketing world to work closely with your "brothers and sisters."

Remember, the customer does not care who says or does what from your communications department. No one wants to know who, in the company, created that great promotion or thought leadership article. They are clearly looking for what they need and the very best experiences with your organization.

Question 44. How Do PR and Sales Fit Together?

If PR works closely with marketing, well then, guess what? PR has to work just as closely with a sales department. PR pros must have a relationship with the sales team. They need access to all your media successes, whether this is in the form of editorial and online coverage, customer success stories, or your favorable product reviews.

At the same time, the sales team should be finding the best customers for the PR team to highlight as client or consumer success stories. They should also share market and customer insights, including any information, reports, statistics, and studies on your industry and competitors. By sharing information and data, the sales team is helping you to be closer to the customer. Knowledge is power. You're also helping salespeople to share the communication tools that build better customer relationships and interest prospects too.

I've always tried to forge relationships with the sales team. When I owned my agency, whenever we won a new account, I would ask for a meeting with the sales team. Our questions included the ones they wanted to hear. To understand and build a relationship with the sales team you need to ask these questions:

1. What are your sales goals?
2. What communication tools do you need from a PR team?
3. What do your customers complain about and what makes them happy?
4. How can we better help to bring customer success stories to light?
5. What's different or interesting that you're hearing from customers or you're doing with your customers?

All these questions immediately tell a sales professional you're there and on the team to help, supporting their efforts from the start.

You can't sit back and wait for someone in your sales department to suggest a meeting. Reach out and set one up yourself. Connect, so PR and sales have the opportunity to meet and work together to benefit the customer.

Question 45. What Does It Mean to be the Ultimate Internal Liaison?

If you're in PR, then you know you're a liaison, managing and facilitating communication, whether it's with the media, customers, different community organizations, analysts, or other external groups. However, your liaison skills will really be tested when you work internally to expand your communication efforts to be more inclusive of all areas of your organization.

Good communication starts on the inside, yet many companies are not connecting their own people to collaborate and learn together. You can use what you know about external communication and connecting people, and then apply the information within your own four walls. Social media is one of the best ways to make those great internal connections and to build cross-functional groups who can tackle challenges and work together. You are the ultimate liaison when you can move beyond your own department to include other areas of the company in collaborative and innovative efforts.

You have a choice. You can stop at liaison, or you can push the limits to become an ultimate liaison, by making a difference on the inside. Technically, what many professionals don't realize is the inside of your company should be the first place to start. The positive steps you make internally in your organization will lead to even stronger and more compelling external communication with the public.

What you do on the inside really shows on the outside.

Question 46. Why Should You Put Your Customer Service Hat on and Keep It on?

From day one of your career to the day you retire, you will be on the customer service team. Everyone, whether you're in PR, marketing, sales, or customer service, should be helping customers when called upon. For example, when a PR person is listed as a "Media" or a "Company" contact on news releases, or in a company newsroom/media center, customers naturally reach out directly thinking you're a part of the customer service team. And, guess what? You are, because you would never turn a customer away. Instead, you would quickly put on your customer service hat to answer their questions, help them on your website, find more product information, or steer them to the appropriate customer service representative.

I remember a conversation dating back to 2002. At the time, I was a VP at my agency and I was also the contact name on JVC news releases. The call came in the late evening when I answered.

> "Hello, this is Deirdre."
> "Hello, Deirdre, can you help me with my JVC GY-DV500?"
> "Sure, how can I assist you?"

"I have a few questions about the repair of my camcorder."
"Okay, I'm happy to help you locate a dealer who can better answer your questions. Do you have access to the JVC Pro website? I'd like to walk you through the process."

This example was back in 2002, pre-dating the proliferation of social media. Today, with everyone making their way to your social media channels, you're also there to listen and to get customers the assistance they need quickly. The goal is to always help as much as you can and then find a customer service representative when the inquiries go beyond your knowledge base. However, at no time would you ever think, "I'm not in Customer Service," or say, "That's not my job."

Without customers, you wouldn't have a job.

Question 47. Why Can't Your Relationships be Perfect?

When you want to build relationships, you have to learn a lot about people. Understanding their needs, challenges, concerns, and agendas should be your first line of focus. However, there will be times when—no matter how much you know, or how well prepared you feel—the relationship is strained. Testy attitudes or tempers can flare up and you find yourself walking on relationship "thin ice." Step back and breathe, because not every negative encounter is about you, or because of something you did. The more pressure your "friends" are under, the more stress they project at you. Unfortunately, you may be in the wrong place at the wrong time.

Whether you encounter an annoyed CEO (Chief Executive Officer), upset supervisor, a less-than-satisfied customer, an overworked colleague, or the journalist on a tight deadline, take any "attitude" and critique with a grain of salt. Listen and acknowledge that you hear what they're saying. Then, use what you hear to learn from the interaction.

I remember one learning experience that stands out in my mind. My agency had been preparing for a media conference for weeks on behalf of our client. The media kits were ready to be handed out to the journalists who attended the event, with about 20 news releases stuffed into them. This was back in the days when journalists still wanted paper releases, although they were also online in the company's newsroom. At one point during the conference, the client (an EVP—Excecutive Vice President—at the company) told a new partner that he was so excited about their newly formed alliance. The EVP went to grab the release about their alliance out of the media kit. Unfortunately, that release received last-minute approval and did not make it into the media kit that day.

As you can imagine the EVP was not happy with our PR team. My team took its lumps accordingly (with me as the lead "lump taker"). Remember, mistakes occur at the top and trickle down. I immediately apologized and said it would not happen again. Eventually, the anger subsided and the relationship with the EVP and our client company continued. This was an example of an imperfect moment, but the relationship went on for many more years. No matter how prepared we thought we were, there was still upset. We learned a lot about our client that day, who felt embarrassed by referencing a release that wasn't physically included in their media kit for him to share. Had we told him the situation in advance, our team, most likely, would have avoided the entire situation.

Your relationships may never be perfect. From the very good interactions to the unpleasant encounters, you will uncover more about the people that matter and their challenges. In the end, you'll be better equipped, and able to strengthen these relationships moving forward.

Question 48. How Do You Handle Rejection?

Rejection is tough. But it serves a great purpose; to make you stronger. Take the media, for example. Yes, no one said it was easy to pitch or to follow up on a news story, knowing you may be shot down very quickly or not even receive an email response. However, rejection is a natural part of any business.

Similar to making mistakes, rejection becomes your opportunity to step back and learn. In the case of the media, you may want to take more time to really understand an outlet's audience and to read the stories written by the journalist on the receiving line. You can also see where journalists hang out on social media. Follow your media contacts on Twitter, and by all means read their blogs, and contribute actively in their communities.

But, rejection is not only reserved for your interactions with the media. You may face rejection when you submit proposals, compete for job promotions, submit creative and business writing, and deliver campaign concepts, to name a few examples. Here's a personal example. Before this book was published, I had about five other book ideas that I pitched, which received absolutely no interest. Whether it was the nature of the topic, the size of the market, the changing nature of the landscape … I've heard it all. But, not once did I say, "That's it, I'm done" (throwing my hands up dramatically) or, "I'm not going to try anymore."

On the contrary, I tried harder. I threw my heart and soul into working on a book project that excited me; one that I wanted to share as a part of my legacy as a communications professional. I've been writing *Answers for Modern Communicators* for many years and finally I connected with the right publishing partner. Sure, I've faced rejection but I've learned from it and then turned my experience into a better opportunity.

Above all, don't take anything personally or give up easily. If you encounter rejection from a journalist or anyone along your career path, then think about what you could have done better. Did you need more detailed information, or would a different type of approach have worked in your favor? Or, maybe this person was just having a bad day.

Make rejection the impetus to try harder, over and over again.

Question 49. Should You Position Yourself as an Expert Source?

If you have expertise in a particular area or subject matter, then offer your counsel to media outlets and blogs. The media and bloggers want to form long-term relationships with professionals who can offer expert commentary, especially when there is breaking news or when hot topics bubble up quickly. Your expert commentary may focus on specific industry knowledge (for example, pharmaceutical, tech, travel, retail, etc.) as a subject-matter expert (SME), or you may have expertise in an industry and comment on broader business matters in the news, such as reputation, branding issues, and crises.

When you provide expert commentary, whether it's in print, online, or in a broadcast interview, the exposure is tremendous for your career growth. Offering yourself may be done through your company or agency connections. Or, it could be as simple as reaching out to specific media and bloggers for a background interview, sharing information about your particular areas of expertise. With all the experts and executives you work with, don't forget your expert self.

For years, I have been doing PR for myself. Today, I work with a publicist who presents angles and story ideas to media outlets that invite me to appear on radio shows, Blog Talk Radio and TV news programs. As you are helping all the experts with their media placements, expert commentary, and building media relationships, don't neglect yourself.

If you devote time and attention to your own PR, then you can be the expert too!

Question 50. How Can You Help Your Executives to Grow?

Your executives are no strangers to speaking, interviewing and being in the public eye. You can be a big part of their growth and success. Make it your job to watch, listen, and offer the gift of feedback. Because you're involved in the company messaging, you know when information is delivered properly and if the appropriate meaning comes across clearly. Because you also have the inside track on the talking points, you're the best candidate to provide valuable commentary to your executives.

When my client was rebranding (after acquiring a tech startup company), we had worked tirelessly with the branding agency on the messaging and talking points for media, analysts, and customers. The COO (Chief Operations Officer) of the company planned to be on stage at the rebrand event to share the exciting news, which was the unveiling of the new brand look, the new leadership, and what this meant for the company's customers. It was the big day and everyone was really excited. I arrived in New York, where the event was taking place, a few hours early. The COO had just finished practicing his short welcome discussion. It was the first time he was using the visuals and sharing the company's story. But, sometimes when you're up on stage and there's no teleprompter, you may miss some important points that need to be articulated. Of course, the audience would never know if you missed something, only the PR person who has worked closely with you.

Now, making the COO feel uncomfortable or anxious is never a good idea right before a big event. You walk a fine line. Plus, we were in a group setting with other executives present, and with no time to pull the COO aside, I didn't want to say, "You forgot one of the most important points that needed to be communicated to your customers." Instead, here's what I said:

> "Your points were solid and your story flowed the whole way through. But, what I also *really* like that you didn't mention was … "

He had a big smile on his face when I shared my feedback and he got the message loud and clear. He later thanked me for helping him fine-tune his talking points and for the gentle reminder.

You can evaluate and share how your executives came across in their interviews, from the answers to questions and important messaging to how they handled some of the unanticipated inquiries. You're there to help them when they need to address their customers or the members of their own team. You're also the one who points out body language signals and if they were making an emotional connection with their audience.

Giving feedback at the executive level is a critical role to play. I always say it is a gift to give and to receive feedback. The key here is growth for professionals, at every level.

Question 51. How Do You Make Your "Friends" Stick Around?

It doesn't matter if you're working with the media, professional colleagues, or business partners. Make it your business to help people so their jobs become a little bit easier. Now, you may be thinking, "What about my job and who's making it more comfortable for me?" What you give, in most cases, is what you will receive in return.

For example, take your relationships with the media. Journalists truly appreciate PR people who answer questions without having to wait a few days searching to find the answers. The best PR people have journalist friends that stick around because they are:

1. responsive to media requests and able to meet the tightest deadlines;
2. proactive and deliver interesting angles to journalists who appreciate the sharing of information before they have to ask;
3. accurate, truthful, and consistently deliver timely information;

Figure 2.2 Make Your Friends Stick Around

4. able to follow up with additional information without the journalist having to ask or to chase after them.

The outcome is having their stories published on deadline. At the same time, you benefit from more impressive coverage. Suddenly, everyone's life just got a little bit easier.

Think about your contacts first and get them what they need. Then, see how this comes back to help you. You may not find immediate benefit all of the time. But, in the end, you will have more people wanting to work with you, many more than the person who does not care enough to make someone else's job a little easier.

Question 52. What Is the Best Way to Get to Know a Journalist or Blogger?

There is a big, ongoing complaint from the media. PR people don't take the time to fully understand a news outlet or know a journalist's specialized area of reporting. When will these complaints stop? With all the intelligence available through search engines and social media communities, and new PR tools that match media influencers to your content, there's no excuse for the useless pitch.

If you don't understand the media outlet or the blog, the types of stories covered, a journalist's interests, and the variety of information their audiences enjoy, then you shouldn't bother reaching out. Here are a few helpful relationship-building hints:

- Read as many stories as you can by journalists/bloggers you want to pitch.

Figure 2.3 Journalist Relationship-Building Tips

- Take a look at archived publications and the type of coverage on a particular topic over a period of time.
- Find out what type of information the journalist/blogger and publication likes to receive and in what format.
- Use search engines to uncover a broader look at where your media contacts are and what they like to do.
- Make sure you connect with them through social media, where it makes sense (caution, not their personal Facebook page).
- Engage with journalists and their communities; be a part of the meaningful conversation.
- Share their stories with your network and tag them in your posts or @mention them in your tweets.
- Give, as a helpful and timely resource, more than you expect to receive, keeping your media contacts updated with news, information, and potential story ideas.

If you take these steps seriously, then moving forward the complaints will no longer be about you. Wouldn't you rather ditch the useless pitch, before someone decides to ditch you?

Question 53. What Happens When You Break a Promise?

If you promise something to the media or any other important group, then you had better deliver. Otherwise, the trust and credibility that you've worked so hard to build fizzles out quickly.

If you're going to make a promise, then you need to take a couple of steps to be sure you can actually deliver on your word.

Step 1: Thoroughly understand what is expected of you.

Step 2: Be aware that time frames are extremely important as professionals are working on tight deadlines. Unlike what you may do for your own marketing communication programs, such as padding deadlines to give people a little more time, this is not necessarily the case for the professionals you work with.

If you find yourself in a situation where you have promised materials, resources, or even an interview with experts and you cannot deliver on time, then reach out as quickly as possible to inform your contact. Unfortunately, in the case of working with the media, they may pass on using your expert the next time around.

However, not every undelivered promise has to end in disaster, depending on how you handle it. I remember working with my client to fill a panel session at the PRSA International Conference back in 2014. We had several influencers who had agreed to participate. A few weeks before the event, I received a call from one of the panelists. His mom had a terrible fall and broke her hip. She was in the hospital and he needed to take care of her. He was very quick to share the information and even offered to help find someone else to fill his shoes. As a result, we were able to shift to our Plan B, which was to find another professional who was already at PRSA to join the group. Luckily within a couple of days we had our new panel member and the conference session was standing room only.

For the sake of your relationships, know what is expected so you can always deliver what you promise. But if you can't, then it is how you handle not being able to fulfill your obligation that will make or break the relationship.

Question 54. Why Is Lying a Relationship Ender?

Here is a short lesson. Lying to the media or any constituent is unacceptable behavior, and has serious consequences, sometimes even legal action against you. Your actions should be based on ethical, credible, and responsible communication. Even the smallest twist of the truth can escalate into big trouble. Don't lie to anyone in your organization, or for anyone, such as a supervisor, partner, peer, friend, etc.

I learned a valuable lesson during my years of agency work. A VP at the agency gave me an envelope to mail. She said, "Please take this to the post office and *don't* put it in the mail slot downstairs in our building." I said, "Sure, I'm happy to do this for you." As I was leaving with the letter in hand, my direct supervisor stopped me and said, "Don't go to the post office, please drop the letter in the mail slot downstairs in the lobby. I need you working on the 'XYZ' event asap; the team has agreed that we need you here."

So, what did I do? I went and dropped the letter in the mailbox downstairs. Well, guess what? I was now a part of a lie, knowing my VP was very clear with her directive. Thankfully, my VP knew enough not to blame the messenger. At the same time, I realized I had to be accountable. Moving forward I would think differently about this type of situation.

If you ever receive conflicting directives, you need make sure both parties who gave the different directives know the steps you are about to take, not just the last person who tells you what to do. For me, this would have meant really knowing if the *entire team* had agreed to how the letter was to be mailed.

Unfortunately, the relationship between my supervisor and VP was never the same from that day forward. Lying will always hurt someone in the end. If you lie or you are involved in a lie, or there are lies swirling around you, then somewhere or somehow a relationship will be severed and everyone involved loses.

Enough said.

Question 55. Do Your Stories Pass the "What's in It for Me" Test?

With the ability to gather, collaborate, and share their own news, information, and entertainment, consumers are in the C-Seat; what I call the Consumer-Seat behind the wheel of their own communication vehicles. They have the control and decide if they want to hear news about you or your business. They say when, what, with whom, and how they're going to collect and share what they like with their own personal networks. With an extremely noisy media landscape, you need to replace your self-serving company announcements with valuable and customized content that is meaningful in your customer's world.

An important first step is to educate anyone in your company who still believes that every piece of "news" is worthy of an announcement. You know better, and now it's time for others in your organization to understand as well. Sometimes your "news" is not even worth a tweet or a Facebook update, let alone a news release distributed over a newswire or a client-wide email. Think about what people want from you ... all your stakeholders.

You have so many choices when it comes to sharing your stories today. Sure, there will be times when your news is mainstream and you will cast a wider net. But, at other times, you can carve out more specific stories for different types of bloggers and influencers, or even share directly with your customers. In every instance, make your news and information customized, valuable, and about them.

Your news has to pass the "What's in it for me" test, which means what you share has to play an important part in your recipient's world. You can build relationships through content, but only if you can deliver meaning and value.

Question 56. What Is the Ratio for Give and Take in a Relationship?

Maintain the attitude that you will give more to your "friends" than you will take from them. Having a great network means helping people; not because you have to, but because you want to make a difference. Giving back to my industry and the professionals who have helped me is a large part of my career today, and it defines my own personal success.

Social media has opened up a whole new way of giving for me, from working with my professional peers to the students who need help with their projects, career advice, and questions about marketing communications. It's one of the reasons this book came to fruition. The questions get more frequent and the communicators come from different countries, through various channels and from professionals of all ages.

A couple of give-back conversations stand out in my mind. I was online with a 69-year-old communicator who asked to "pick my brain" about book writing and publishing. He also shared some interesting stories about his life's work. I shared my approach and process, and at the end of the conversation I walked away believing that he would write his memoir one day. On that same day, two middle school students contacted me through email about their National History

Day project. They wanted me to participate in an interview to share my thoughts on social media and the gay rights movement. From the seasoned veteran to younger, school-age children my giving was not predicated on receiving anything in return.

This level of giving back is not new. Many professionals are right there with me helping, sharing, and doing their part. However, some may think the number of connections through social media and the amount of insights that you are asked to share is far too time-consuming. On the contrary, I believe there are tremendous rewards for helping people and seeing them achieve their goals over time. The best type of thank you and the greatest gratification come when you see people achieving their dreams.

When you give back enough to the industry and your colleagues, eventually the "universe" and all your connections will start to recognize you in bigger ways. Then, as you build up your continued career successes, it is an even bigger opportunity for you to give more.

As you think about how you will give back and build relationships, ask yourself a question. If everyone decided to stop sharing insights because it was too time-consuming, then where would you be today?

Question 57. How Do You Maintain Your Networking?

You should not place limits on growing your network of professional contacts. Just because you have many great relationships doesn't mean you have to stop pursuing valuable connections. Not only will you continue to meet interesting people, but you'll also be able to stay up to date with industry information and insights from your new acquaintances.

The key is to network and scale. Know and respect that there are levels of relationships. You have to select the right contacts, matching the opportunities that make the most sense for you and your connections to pursue at a certain point in time. Not everyone will move to a level of new business venture, partnership, or trusted resource. As you move up the relationship staircase, relationships will grow and change and some may stall and fade.

Feeding your connections pipeline through networking will ensure that you have a rich database of contacts available to you at all times and at varying levels of "friendship." Your pipeline should always be full and your opportunities plentiful. Similar to the saying, "You shouldn't put all of your eggs in one basket," you want to maintain your level of networking for the same reason.

So, by all means diversify and grow your connections, and pull them from different relationship baskets when you need them.

Question 58. How Do You Make Your First Meeting Really Count?

The potential for a relationship to grow starts with the very first meeting. If you have the opportunity to meet with someone in your network, whether it is via a telephone call, Skype, or in-person meeting, then you should prepare as if it were your first job interview. Imagine the possibilities if professionals treated every meeting as if it were their first interview. There would be an increased potential for stronger bonds and more valuable outcomes.

Of course, this approach requires extra effort on your part. However, it is well worth the time and energy. When you really prepare for a meeting, you are saying that you care about who is in the meeting, and you want to advance the relationship. Doing your homework and understanding everything about the people who are participating and what they care about are extremely important steps.

However, it is not just about what happens in the meeting and that first great impression. You also have to think about your meeting follow up. What are the follow-up steps to advance the relationship to the next phase? Here are a few follow-up best practices that will enable you to show initiative and interest:

1. Write a meeting follow-up note, thanking a professional for taking the time to meet/Skype or chat by phone. My personal favorite is the handwritten note. It is an older practice that really gets a person's attention.
2. If there are follow-up materials discussed or requested during the meeting, let a professional know your time frame for delivering the information or send it immediately.
3. Ask a professional if there is anything else they need from you or if they have any additional questions not covered in your meeting.
4. Drop a note from time to time, not to request something but just to offer information of value or to congratulate them on their

accomplishments (LinkedIn is a great community that enables you to keep in touch).

5. Share a professional's work actively through your social networks and let her know you appreciate her insights and expertise.

When you think about every meeting on a higher level and the follow up that is involved, you raise the bar on your relationships. For me, building relationships is more than a skill, it is at the heart of my career. Every great relationship starts with your focus and how you approach the first meeting.

Question 59. How Does Visualizing Your Connections Grow a Relationship?

Social media has you connecting in any number of communities. However, participating in a community is not about your number of friends and followers. On the contrary, it is understanding how and why you are connected, the like-mindedness of the people you are attracting, and the context of your discussions.

Using visualization software to see your network connections helps you to uncover who is the most actively involved in your community conversations. Their level of interaction with you, from initial participation to more meaningful engagement, reveals the people who have the most interest in what you're saying, and in what you're doing and sharing. Visualizing your connections helps you to grow any relationship based on what people experience with you and how they prefer to interact with you.

Here is an example of how visualization helped to build relationships with food bloggers when we were launching a new restaurant gift card experience. We needed to find foodies who would be willing to participate at our launch by receiving the gift card, using it at a restaurant, and then writing about the experience to interest their online communities. Because of a very short time frame, it was easier to find food bloggers through our own personal connections than it was to build a list of top tier bloggers and pitch them blindly.

Using a simple Twitter tool called Mentionmapp, we looked at the members of our own team on Twitter, and who they engaged in food conversations. We uncovered several close connections who were frequently engaging with foodies or food bloggers in these tightly woven influencer circles. In a very short time frame, we were able to find a handful of food bloggers who were connected to our close friends. Through easy introductions from our close friends, these bloggers were pitched and happily accepted our invitation to participate in the gift card program. These very same bloggers also recommended some of their own friends, who were also bloggers who wanted to participate in the restaurant gift card experience. Our ten bloggers quickly quadrupled our pool, which led to a very successful campaign and many product reviews and endorsements.

When you see the relationship, you can find creative ways to grow it—directly or indirectly.

Question 60. How Do You Cultivate Relationships Locally and Globally?

The best relationships are only as good as the time you put into them. Time and effort equate to stronger bonds. Technology allows you to connect, share, and collaborate more closely, getting to know people long before you meet them in person. In addition, social media lets you transcend borders and boundaries. You are as local as you want and as global as you prefer to be.

Years ago, you would have to wait to see your colleagues and peers at an annual industry event. Today, you can see anyone at any time, and time zones are no longer an inconvenience. Cultivating your connections, and getting to know other professionals better, is as quick as a Skype video call, or sharing a link to a Join.me meeting. You can set up a GoToMeeting or jump into a Google+ hangout. Now, I look forward to chatting with my friends in Spain, England, and the Netherlands. I had one client who was a digital nomad, traveling from city to city every month. Connecting via Skype every week made our working relationship stronger than if we were just chatting by phone.

You are no longer bound to networking or even work restrictions. Instead, you can connect and cultivate your local connections, while you develop a much stronger global network.

Question 61. What Constitutes "Stalking" Tactics or Acceptable Boundaries?

There is a fine line between researching the people you want to get to know and discovering too much information about them personally. Of course, when it comes to the media most journalists like how PR people take the time to understand as much about their past stories and even personal pitching preferences. But, be careful not to go overboard to the point that it looks like you're some kind of stalker. Knowing about contacts works professionally but not personally, unless they invite you into their personal circle of friends.

You walk a fine line with all the information you uncover at your fingertips. Think about what you would want people to know about you as you're building a relationship. Anything you think is borderline uncomfortable for you should be considered off limits. Researching to the point of looking like a creepy new friend will get you ignored or blocked immediately.

When someone connects to me, it is an opportunity to make a first impression. I'm only just meeting and getting to know this fellow community member. At this point, making any kind of comment about my very attractive daughter on Instagram (in more colorful words, of course), is definitely a boundary crossed right there. A little too much homework on my family and me!

Question 62. Who Is the Trusted Confidant?

At the top of the relationship staircase is the trusted confidant who you will trust with sacred information. Together, you can safely bounce around new ideas, share concepts, and even learn more about yourself in a safe, judgment-free zone. A trusted confidant can give and take positive feedback, as well as a negative critique. Their help and the trust you have together is always balanced and appreciated.

At times, the trusted confidant is someone whom you may communicate with frequently or that friend/professional who weaves in and out of your life at important intervals. However, you always know you have a trustworthy source and sounding board. These individuals have your best interest at heart, as you have theirs. They are a part of your trusted advisory board on topics and information that you would not find easily or that is not readily available to you.

I will never forget what one of my trusted confidants told me. We met in New York City one beautiful day in May when she was visiting the east coast for business. I was having one of those challenging months. As I was navigating some ups and downs, I mentioned that no matter the situation, I would survive. Being a confidant, she stopped me and stated, "I don't want you to just survive, you need to thrive." These words stuck with me ever since that day. Only a trusted confidant can offer this type of advice.

The trusted confidant is the type of relationship that comes few and far between. If you are fortunate enough to have a trusted confidant, then you should cherish this very special relationship.

The Experts Weigh In

Jennifer Connelly, CEO, JConnelly

Invest in People

Many tools promise to manage and build relationships.

Email, texting, audio messages, tweets, Siri, Snapchat, FaceTime, LinkedIn, and Tinder are all available from your phone, your tablet, your car, while watching TV, or in the shower.

Technology certainly improves our ability to instantaneously share information ("Look at the salad I just had for lunch!"), but it fails to genuinely connect us.

In our hyper-connected modern society, many people crave something more. For example, when I meet someone in business and want to develop a real relationship, I send a quick, warm email after our meeting, but then I'll follow up with a handwritten note or a carefully chosen book that is relevant to something we discussed.

Relationships need to be nurtured.

People who desire genuine relationships are often givers and if you are a giver, then you'll find yourself in situations that can blossom. When I was a young account manager, I was handed a client on the verge of firing my agency. Rather than dismiss the client, I dug into understanding why the relationship was in crisis and what I could do to solve those issues. Then I began the work of regaining the client's trust—effectively turning that relationship around. Today, that client remains an important part of my life, personally and professionally.

At the time, I had no idea how the future would unfold, but I believed that if I took the time to help, without any expectation of a quid pro quo, and just made deposits into the bank of goodwill, I would form a genuine meaningful relationship.

And I did.

Uninterrupted face time is sacred. Just the simple act of eating with another person and enjoying good food and drink will create a genuine opportunity to form a more meaningful relationship. And keep your phone off the table! I think it's rude to even have the phone visible—a reminder that at any given second, the person across the table might become less important than whatever might beep, buzz, or flash on your phone.

Make the time. Telling yourself that you are too busy is no excuse. Everyone is too busy. I actually start by blocking out time on my calendar for meals and quality time, even before I've figured out with whom I'll spend that time. Weekly, I share a meal of some sort with as many as ten people, either one-on-one, or with a small group. It's often the most rewarding, enriching, and productive part of my week.

We need to get back to the basics of genuine human interactions.

Take the time to look people in the eye, slow down and ask questions, and then really listen to what a person has to say. It's time to put down the phones and show respect for the person in front of you.

After all, people are not gadgets; let's not treat each other as if we're disposable or interchangeable.

Peter Shankman, Author, Speaker, Founder of Shankminds

Relationships Built to Last

Let's face it, I know a thing or two about growing relationships. I started Help a Reporter Out, the largest website in the world connecting journalists and sources. I build HARO because, for as long as I can remember, I'd been very good at one specific thing:

Connecting people. I'm very, very curious. I enjoy finding out about people. Let's face it—if I'm on a plane next to you, unless you fake your death, I'm going to know a lot about you by the time we land.

I enjoy connecting people. I enjoy the little thrill that comes with introducing two people (or more) and watching great things come from that introduction. And it's because of that my relationships are built to last. Simply put, I put out ten times more help into the universe than I ask for. That's how you make relationships last.

Everyone has that one friend who only reaches out when they need something. Annoying, huh? I'm the opposite. Chances are, I reach out to you when I don't need anything. I reach out when I have something to *offer.* Perhaps it's an article I found that matches one of your interests, or perhaps it's a photo of something I think you might enjoy. The point is, I'm taking the time to reach out and say "Hi," with a little tidbit that you didn't expect, that doesn't require anything in return and, even better, makes you smile. I'm putting help out there into the universe. That creates positivity. It strengthens a relationship. Whether it's a reporter, or a business contact, or a client, or a potential customer.

The best part? I'm not simply doing something for the sake of getting something in return. I'm being genuinely helpful, because I believe that's the right way to be. Real relationships, strong relationships, relationships that stand the test of time, should be based on mutual respect and growth. That's how I grow my relationships.

Valerie Simon, VP of Communications, Atlantic Health System

Develop Business Relationships that Are Meaningful and Enduring

Business relationships are often classified as "contacts" or "connections." They can be defined by a specific association, such as a common workplace or industry, with the purpose of mutual collaboration for a temporary period of time. Developing business relationships that are both meaningful and enduring requires a significant investment, but can yield unexpected and tremendous returns.

Put people first: In striving to reach the aims of the business, it is easy to ignore what is most important. For every exercise designed to achieve a business return, there are opportunities to impact those around you. Consider how those on your team might grow, learn, and prosper from the experience. Will those who work alongside you be able to look back and say they personally profited from your efforts? Are they better for having known you?

Stay engaged: Use social media, email, your phone, or even an old-fashioned letter. Don't limit yourself to simply acknowledging birthdays, promotions, and awards. Actively seek opportunities to reach out. Forward an article or information that could be of interest, share an upcoming event, or ask them for their opinion on a project or idea. Likewise, be sure to respond to their communications thoughtfully and in a timely manner. Show them that you value the relationship.

Be both a rock star and a fan: Add value and share your talents, but don't hold back when it comes to celebrating others. Recognizing strengths and expertise in others does not diminish your own authority.

Don't be limited by a business title or affiliation: It can be okay to blur the line between personal and professional. Respecting the privacy of others and using good judgment and discretion in the workplace is necessary; however, developing meaningful relationships requires a willingness to be personal. Make an effort to learn more about the people you work with. Strive to understand what matters most to them. Our value to others extends beyond what they may find on a business card or resume.

Do what's right, not what's easy: Navigating business objectives, office politics, and limitations on time and financial resources will present inevitable challenges. How you treat people during the most trying times will leave the greatest impression.

Joe Provenza, CIO, Flagler College

Data Is Important, but Only Because Relationships Are Critical

At small private colleges, student success and retention are more critical than ever. As such, colleges invest a lot in data analysis tools to help identify students who may be at risk of transfer or dropping out of school altogether. We look at data that helps identify the type of student that we should recruit; that is, who has the best chance of succeeding at our institution. Data can tell us how to best advise our students on how to manage their academic careers. It can also tell us how the students think of themselves.

All of this is very important to the well-being and survival of a small college. However, the success or failure of these data-driven initiatives depends on how they are used and I will give the answer before the question: Data must be used with the students' well-being first and foremost on our minds. If we miss that, we become impersonal and our students become things instead of people. If, however, we use that data to best know our students in order to best take care of them, then both we and our students will succeed.

Despite the fact that my job at the college is to run the technology operation, I signed up to be a first-year advisor. This is a program where staff members are assigned a small number of freshmen advisees (I only ever have four) for their first year at school. The primary role is to advise them academically, and for that I use all of the aforementioned data. However, I never learned the trick of using data to only tell me when they were in trouble, or to tell them what class to take next. I use it to know as much about them as I can so that I can best take care of them in every way possible. You see, a student going away for the first time is a little more apprehensive than they let on. Their parents are usually terrified. I almost feel personally responsible for them; but I've really just met them. Enter all the data that we have gathered and I have a head start in communicating with them to establish the kind of relationship that builds trust and lets them know that I genuinely care.

I could give you examples in which I have turned a student's academics and/or their future at our college around, but the example I will share is one in which we actually lost a student to another institution because it best illustrates the point.

Frieda (not her real name) showed up as a very bright, academically qualified, and energetic student. But one thing I learned from the information that we had, and from my first meeting with her, was that she would be prone to homesickness. And, she was far from home. When she came in for the first meeting, I knew I might be hearing this from her and was prepared to address the issue. We were quickly able to get to the heart of some of her concerns and I was able to frame the decision she was trying to make, such that she knew all of the implications of either choice.

In the end, she chose to go to a school near her home and, after it was all said and done, it was the best choice for her. On her last day, I had her whole family in my office for a tearful goodbye. Her parents were extremely grateful and I am still in touch with them and with the student. The benefit to the student is obvious. The benefit to the College is reputation. We may have lost a student that we were going to lose anyway, but not without them knowing how much we care. They left thinking and saying that our school was a most amazing place (it just wasn't located in their home state). So, we may enroll several other students based on the testimony of people who know how much we care for our students. But, even if we don't in this case, we took care of a student like we said we would.

In higher education, it begins and ends with sincere relationships (with a little data sprinkled in the middle, and that only to make the relationships better).

Notes

1 Deirdre Breakenridge and Tom DeLoughry, *The New PR Toolkit, Strategies for Successful Media Relations* (Harlow: Financial Times Prentice Hall Books, February 2003).
2 Deirdre Breakenridge, *Social Media and Public Relations, Eight New Practices for the PR Professional* (New York: FT Press, May 2012).

Chapter 3

Socializing Your Brand

For me, being "social" used to mean networking at industry events and taking time to cultivate relationships in person. Years ago, as an agency owner, I would go to a marketing or PR function once a week and also make a point of catching up with colleagues by telephone or over lunch. However, the meaning of being social today, or socializing your brand, has expanded; it's a complete game changer for the modern communicator. When social media entered onto the business scene, many communicators faced a harsh reality. They were *not* ready to take a truly social approach to communication, which was online, peer-like, collaborative, open and transparent, and much more human than ever before. Building relationships in these quickly proliferating social media communities was a whole different world.

Social media opened up what many called the "corporate kimono" and required PR and marketing to "listen" to conversations and to figure out the best ways to be genuine. Sharing news stories had to be customized and not considered an interruption. Information had to be delivered in a more meaningful manner. Today, socializing your brand means that you have to adjust your storytelling, content creation, and engagement to meet the socially accepted ways of community sharing. If done correctly, companies and their communicators have the unique opportunity to get closer to their customers and to become more valuable resources to many different groups.[1]

Socializing your brand does not mean being in hundreds of communities and just expanding for the sake of having a presence. On the contrary, wherever you have a presence, you have to be an active participant. This takes time and resources. When you socialize your brand, you do it with purpose and you become an important contributor to your communities. Early on, many communicators were criticized for how they jumped into social media without really understanding the culture and the norms of the different networks and platforms. They were quickly labeled as spammers or blacklisted by bloggers and journalists. When you socialize your brand the right way, the word spam doesn't exist in your vocabulary. You're building relationships with people who have similar interests and values, and you're managing your participation at the same time.

In this chapter, the questions and answers presented will help you to socialize your brand in such a way that people will not only care about what you say, but they'll also want to engage with you as friends and peers. Socializing your brand is an opportunity to create stronger bonds. For your company, it means more loyal customers and advocates.

Question 63. How Do You Know Where to Hang Out on Social Media?

One important social media rule to remember ... if people are talking about you, your company, and the topics related to your area of expertise, then there's a good reason for you to explore your digital presence. But, you need to do more than just know where they are and listen intently to these discussions. You also have to be aware of the culture, and the values and norms of every community to participate effectively. Before you join the conversation, take the time to understand how your audience interacts, what they like to share, and why they would want to interact with you.

Remember, being a part of a community means adding value and helping someone by sharing what is important to them. The concept of community always involves peer-to-peer engagement and supporting people. If you can think about the meaning of community and helping your peers, then you'll be able to hang out comfortably, when and where it matters. You'll be considered a welcomed addition by any of your social media "friends."

Back in 2008, I decided to hang out in a Facebook group with some tech peers. I didn't participate right away, but instead watched the group interactions. Finally, when one of the group members had a question about mining data and intelligence gathering, I jumped into the discussion to share a good resource. By answering this question, and being helpful, I forged a new relationship with a director of IT services for one of the largest food manufacturers in the world. After connecting her with a few more of my personal contacts, she reached out to me privately. She asked me if I would consider working with her team on an internal, collaborative social media project for their company. Socializing your brand pays off!

This was a good lesson for two reasons:

1. When you find the right groups, because you understand the culture and behavior, you can help others.
2. When you help others, you're seen as a valuable resource, which may turn into a reciprocal opportunity.

As you expand your digital footprint, you too can be a welcomed addition to any community as long as you're willing to help.

Question 64. How Do You Take "Listening" to a Whole New Level?

Social media gives you the incredible opportunity to become more intimate with the people you care about. You can use social media monitoring (free or paid tools) to "listen" closely or monitor conversations in different communities using keywords related to your company, products, executives, competitors, and the marketplace. You can also hear how people feel about you and your own professional brand. There is no shortage of information or opinions shared.

The more time you invest in your monitoring or "listening," the more you will learn to share what is meaningful to others and create the types of engagement that make a difference. Listening first also helps you to create communication to stand out and distinguish yourself. Your job is to give people what they need. Listening closely helps you to identify and answer questions or concerns, and create and distribute valuable content when and exactly where they want it.

I built my blog, PR Expanded, and wrote most of my books by uncovering the critical pain points experienced by communicators on Twitter. I would follow different hashtags (#PRTech, #PRStudChat, #CrisisManagement, #SocialMedia, #PublicRelations, #PRjobs, #Reputation, etc.) and different combinations of PR keywords. Then, I created articles to answer the communication questions and to solve the pressing issues.

Whether it was my own approach to a problem or I interviewed other experts and influencers for their perspectives, my content always addressed the pertinent issues PR and marketing pros discussed. Eventually, an abundance of ideas and pillars of thought leadership turned into several books.

I remember attending a conference just after my book, *Social Media and Public Relations*, was published. A well-known PR blogger raised his hand during the Q&A portion of my presentation. He said, "What you've just presented in your keynote really crystallized what we've all been saying, wanting, and asking for over the years."

Exactly what I was hoping to hear. That's how you can take "listening" to a whole new level.

Question 65. Do You Have to be Everywhere on Social Media?

For today's modern communicator, digital and social media are not a communication option; they are a communication must. Regardless of your age, or experience, opportunity will pass you by quickly if you're not aware of and knowledgeable about the "new" social media platforms, tools, and resources for your company and your own professional development.

However, there is only so much time in a day to be effective through your social channels. The key is to understand that you, personally, don't have to be everywhere. But, for your company, you may have to spend more time becoming familiar and conversant when it comes to the new tools, resources, and apps that interest your customers.

For example, I don't have a Periscope account. But, when Periscope launched, I did my homework, researching and discussing the platform with many of its users. I took the time to understand the opportunities for brands, talking directly to different groups about live streaming and knowing why, when, and how businesses could use Periscope effectively.

At the same time, if you asked me if I would be streaming video live via Facebook years ago, I may have said, "What for?" Now, it's an imperative for some of my clients. As a part of my work with them, I'm on Facebook Live interviewing experts and sharing information at their tradeshow events and conferences. I've also personally dabbled in Facebook Live to share interesting new adventures. For example, when I recorded my third Lynda.com and LinkedIn Learning video course, I took the opportunity to share the news on Facebook Live. I interviewed my course producer and director. It was a great way to reach over 7,700 people who might be interested in my course.

If you play a role in your company's communication, targeting different groups (internal or external), then learning new technology is now a part of your job description. You certainly don't have to be everywhere, but you do have to know a lot about different communication channels.

Question 66. Is It Important to Learn a Social Media Vocabulary?

Communicators need to adopt a new language, or an updated vocabulary, in order to "fit" into different social media communities, and the discussions that ensue. Otherwise, you may stick out like a sore thumb. The goal is to become a member of the network and to seamlessly adapt to its language and culture.

For example, if you're spending time on Twitter, then you would know the best practices when it comes to:

- direct messages (DMs)
- @ replies
- mentions
- pinned tweets
- promoted tweets
- quoted re-tweets
- tweet chats
- hashtags.

And, if you spend time on Instagram, then you would want to familiarize yourself with:

- feed
- filters
- caption
- hashtags
- Instagram direct
- stories
- geotags
- Instagram apps.

Every social community has specific terms of engagement that you will need to know to participate successfully and to blend in with your peers. The same goes for Snapchat, Reddit, or any other social community where you decide to participate. Platforms may launch and fail. So, no matter where you are, what's important to remember is there is a community and a language built into the culture.

Learning a new language and growing your social media glossary will help you in your social conversations and interactions. Of course, if you build your glossary be sure to share it with other colleagues and peers so they can learn too. The more you can be collaborative and educate one another, the more you will grow professionally and propel your industry forward.

Question 67. Do PR Pros Need Creative Independence?

Years ago, PR people were recognized in their organizations as the writers and the storytellers. However, when they needed different visuals, photography, website designs, and video footage to accompany their stories, they relied upon illustrators, designers, photographers, videographers, etc., for their imagery and multimedia needs. The times have certainly changed. Today, you can create your own websites, blogs, photos, infographics, memes, videos, etc.

Creative tools are abundant and easy-to-access resources. They offer you everything from royalty-free images to downloadable design templates, with step-by-step directions to create and share your reports, newsletters, infographics, posters, presentations, and more. You no longer have to wait for someone else to create images or designs on your behalf.

To get into the "discover, design, and create" mode, you can rely on a number of easy-to-access sources:

- Conduct a quick YouTube video search to help you find videos on creating your own visual designs. YouTube is the second largest search engine next to Google.
- Research different free or cost-effective design tools through search engines or ask your peers for recommendations.
- Open up discussions on Twitter, Facebook, and in your LinkedIn groups to learn about creative tools. This is how I learned about Piktochart, Canva, and Pablo by Buffer.
- Take a quick poll to find out which creative tools your friends and colleagues prefer. Your peers will be more than willing to share and rate their favorites for creative storytelling. At the same time, you'll learn which resources are the easiest to navigate, offer the most creative design options, and are worth the time or dollar investment.

Figure 3.1 Get into Your Discover, Design, and Create Mode

In addition to being an excellent writer, you can now design and create attention-grabbing visuals. Your hands-on use of powerful imagery will further ignite your storytelling.

When you are using tools to design and create visuals or videos, then you have reached creative independence status.

Question 68. How Do You Move from Tech Tester to Tech Specialist?

I talk a lot about PR Tech Testers. These are professionals who take the time to research, test, and implement technology as a part of their daily PR function.[2] These pros are great at technology exploration and they're naturally skilled at expanding their social media presence. However, as a modern communicator, you should not stop at simple tech testing.

Because technology continues to change the media landscape, your role requires you to advance into a whole new technology realm. You have the opportunity to evolve into an even more intimate tech role by mastering social media strategically. For example, the PR Tech Specialist goes beyond testing and knows how to use technology for research, planning, campaign execution through new channels, and measurement that demonstrates the value of communication programs.

You can be more strategic about using technology when you ask these questions:

- How will the technology support my purpose and does it help me to accomplish my goals and objectives?
- Does the technology allow me to take a deeper dive into data intelligence (e.g., ad hoc searches) to better understand my audience?

- What internal resources are available to manage the technology?
- Does the technology cast a wide net or is it for a specific channel?
- Will the technology support our content development and curation process?
- Does the technology offer metrics/measurement and any type of reporting function?

The difference between Tech Tester and Tech Specialist is distinct. The Tech Tester uncovers and experiments with new technology to feel out possible digital expansion and new interactions with stakeholders. But the true Tech Specialist has in-depth knowledge, deeper experience, and a more strategic approach to using new technologies for facilitating better relationships. The result: Stronger relationships with happy customers and loyal advocates.

When you make this critical transition and you graduate to Tech Specialist, you also become recognized as a more valuable asset to your company.

Question 69. How Do You Close the Gap between Communications and Technology?

In business, the Chief Information Officer (CIO) has to work with the Chief Marketing Officer (CMO), and everyone below these two leaders must do the same.

Do you think the frenzied world of marketing communication can work with the precise and logical world of IT, in harmony and without the loss of productivity? The answer is "Yes," and you have to learn how. But, you have to socialize with your tech or IT peers to help close the gap between the two groups.

Working in different organizations, I've discovered a three-part process that must be embraced to close the deep divide:

1. The first part of the process requires breaking out of your communications "silo." Become more integrated and social with other areas of your company. Working together is a large part of what communication requires today.
2. The second part is to roll up your sleeves to learn new social technologies, web analytics, CRM software, and to analyze data and trends. With a new understanding of data, you'll be

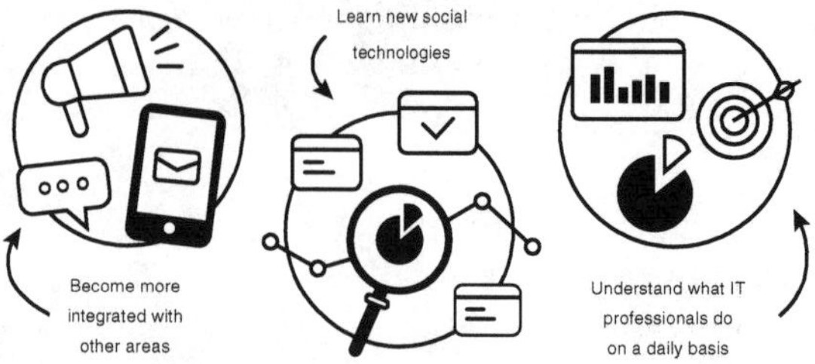

Figure 3.2 Breaking Work Silos

able to better speak their language and learn more about their world.

3. The third and final part of the process is to have a concrete understanding of what IT and tech professionals do on a daily basis and to appreciate their requests and challenges. When you take the time to learn about them, the requests you receive from them will make more sense and vice versa.

Remember, you and your tech counterparts have different jobs, processes, and procedures. But you're all on the same team and, hopefully, now speaking a similar language. Plus, there is one overarching common goal. Everyone, in every department of your company, is working to reach higher-level objectives for the business and to make your customers happy.

Question 70. What Does It Mean to Take the Best of "Traditional" Forward?

What is traditional PR and marketing anyway? Perhaps, in ten years, what may seem like shiny objects in social media and mobile marketing right now will be seen as "traditional" communication or even as obsolete. As a communicator, I've experienced the launch and downfall of Friendster, MySpace, Orkut, Ping, Google Wave, and, at the time of this writing, Vine.

Now take a look at what's happened in PR. First there was PR, then PR 1.0 and PR 2.0. I know because I wrote the book, *PR 2.0 New Media, New Tools, New Audiences*. I stopped counting at PR 3.0 even though colleagues still discuss PR 3.0 as what's next. Why did I stop counting? Because PR is PR, and good PR carries forward the best of its traditional roots.

No matter what technology is preferred and what new media channels and platforms have surfaced, good PR is:

- practicing ethical communication with your internal and external stakeholders;
- planning programs with measureable goals and objectives;
- building a better image or reputation for the health of the brand;
- creating more meaningful and innovative customer experiences;
- sharing news, information, and storytelling that results in customer loyalty and advocacy;
- developing strategic communication to create mutually beneficial, long-term relationships;
- helping to optimize marketing programs that drive leads and company sales.

Technology will continue to facilitate new ways to connect and to create engagement. Whether you're in PR, marketing, or advertising, etc., you have to learn to move the best of traditional methods forward. It doesn't matter what year, what number, or what type of technology is used. Your goal is the health and well-being of the business and the public you serve.

Question 71. What Does Increasing Your Digital Footprint Really Mean?

Increasing your digital footprint means expanding your professional brand online and through social media. It is the sum total of all of your online media and your community participation, including status updates, reviews, search results, and any other content created by you or the content someone else creates about you. Remember, your digital footprint is what others say and post on your behalf, whether you like what they share or not.

When you expand your digital footprint, it is an opportunity to let others know what you stand for; a means to showcase your values and area of expertise, building your reputation and credibility. When you expand your digital footprint the right way there are many benefits including more of the right relationships, industry recognition, and greater credibility, as well as rewarding partnerships.

However, brand building should start long before your professional career begins. Students need to think about their brands prior to graduation. For students, the benefits are tremendous. They include:

- more networking with industry professionals;
- better career opportunities as you meet interesting people;
- alignment with peers who share common interests;
- increased knowledge sharing with your peers;
- tremendous learning potential by accessing new resources/groups;
- credibility in your field, even before you graduate;
- perceived potential to succeed among peers and professionals.

At the same time, while you are brand building and increasing your digital footprint, you must constantly be monitoring your own brand. Using search engines and alerts, you can uncover what is being said about you, from the positive to the negative, always working diligently to turn negative sentiment into a positive learning experience.

Increasing your footprint means greater opportunity but also translates into brand monitoring and more responsibility. You are giving people the permission to review, learn, and discuss you even more, based on the information you have shared.

Question 72. When Should You Update Your PR and Marketing Toolkit?

You should update your PR and marketing toolkit frequently because tools, resources, and apps are constantly changing. Your toolkit should consist of the tested and trusted tools that you need to do your job effectively.

In 2003, my book the *The New PR Toolkit* discussed toolkits ten plus years ago. At the time a PR toolkit included surveys, polls, news releases, print and digital media kits, fact sheets, email, newsletters, clipping services, dark crisis websites, and online newsrooms, to name a few important kit components.

However, your toolkit today expands to reflect an age of social conversations and the proliferation of social media communities. Of course, you're probably still using surveys, polls, news releases, digital media kits, fact sheets, email, newsletters, etc. However, the more socialized communicator's toolkit must be armed with:

- monitoring/tracking tools to listen to what your customers and other important constituents are saying;
- authority/ranking tools to find the influencers or influential individuals that will help you to amplify messages and create action among target audiences;
- highly customized content and targeted stories to reach your community members;
- company/blogger ethics and guidelines and social media policies for better community participation;
- web analytics to capture unique visitors, page views, bounce rates, referral traffic, time spent on a page, etc.;
- a host of social media tools, resources, and apps to consider for content creation and curation;
- a new guide to metrics and data explaining the difference between capturing ROI (Return on Investment) as it relates to your business goals and objectives, as well as what metrics are used to track exposure, engagement, preference, etc.

Your toolkit should reflect the changing times and new media technology. It should showcase what's new and relevant in technology. When your toolkit relates directly to your customer's news and information-gathering habits, and content sharing preferences, then your tools will create the most meaningful brand experiences to excite them.

Question 73. When It Comes to Social Media, Should You Just Ask a Millennial?

Talking to Millennial consumers takes the guesswork out of social media. Remember, a Millennial may not have a few decades of business experience. However, these up-and-coming pros have been exposed to disruptive technology as a part of their schooling, and have learned about and used social media at an early age.

For example, according to the studies on Snapchat, I'm clearly not the popular demographic.[3] Of course, as a communication professional, it is my job to learn, understand, and be able to help companies when they ask questions about new social media channels and apps. The first place I turn to is my Millennial connections.

Whether I use my own "built-in" family focus group, or I learn from younger professionals in my Twitter and Facebook communities, asking is the only way to get the inside scoop.

If you want to learn why the younger generation are addicted to a social media community, or a new app, then you have to do some reverse mentoring. When you are helping them, turn the table and ask some questions. They are more than happy to share why they love Snapchat, Reddit, and YouTube. At the same time, if you plan to participate in a community that skews younger, then make sure your team is comprised of younger professionals who understand both the technology and the culture of the community because they are active themselves.

There's a reason why the clothing brand, Wet Seal, gave their Snapchat account to a 16-year-old blogger. After they saw an increase of about 9,000 new friends, they knew they needed the help of a younger digital native to fit in and engage in ways that they may not have done on their own.[4]

Question 74. How Can You be More Strategic about Your Communication?

For me, the best part of being a modern communicator is the strategy part. Directly related to the strategist role is access to tremendous amounts of data and analytics that show important trends. When you can tap into data and analytics, you're able to work smarter, communicate more effectively, and be much more in-tune with your company, customers, and the market.

At one time, I was a communicator who, pre-Internet, was pushing papers, buried in books and various print resources. My primary or first-hand research and the discovery process for a client account took a much different form than it does today. Now, technology provides you with readily available information online. The speed at which you can obtain the information continues to increase.

However, keep in mind that an incredibly dynamic public tied to their mobile devices feeds the data surge. People are more than willing to share ideas, thoughts, emotions, and even personal preferences freely and at all times of the day and night. Among the many groups talking are your customers. They want to interact, co-create and crowdsource with their favorite brands. They want to feel closer and be more a part of the company or your product experience ... if you let them.

You actually have two of the greatest sources for your research and planning:

1. The data you gather from the direct collaborative interactions you have feed into your strategy.
2. The people who give you feedback openly and directly and what you experience together make you more strategic.

Being a strategist today requires capturing the data, analyzing it for trends and understanding, and engaging directly to learn through the experiences of your customers.

Question 75. Does Digging Deeper into Social Media Give You a Competitive Edge?

Your competition is sharing information and you don't always need expensive tools to understand them and to stand out in a different way. But you have to dig deeper. Looking on the surface will only give you surface knowledge.

You can use social media to gain intelligence by watching, tracking, and evaluating competitor interactions. Of course, it is easy to check out how many followers your competitors have, and the lists where they appear (all on the surface). And, yes, you can also scour through their friends and followers to see which important influencers they have connected with and their resulting levels of engagement. Even a Google search is considered surface intelligence today.

However, there are a few less obvious ways to figure out if your competitors are just getting their feet wet, or if they are farther along with a communications and social media strategy. Ask yourself a few questions:

- Do they have a clear branding and messaging strategy that is consistent and focused throughout their social media channel?
- Are they using dedicated links to landing pages to track social media engagement and activity?
- Are they timing all their tweets or engaging frequently with people in real time?
- Do they have a community manager or a group of community managers for their social media properties?
- Does social media stop on weekends and holidays?

Another great way to tell if your competitors are socializing their brands the right way is whether they have active employee champions who amplify messages. Do they have a unified army of internal brand ambassadors? You can also study the content they deliver through their channels to determine how their audiences react to what they share.

Lastly, if your competitors are crowdsourcing with community members, then they're hitting the highest levels of engagement with their brand enthusiasts. If you want to check out a couple of good examples of crowdsourcing, there's Mike's Hard Lemonade and AT&T.

Mike's Hard Lemonade crowdsources their Mike's Harder Lemonade brand. This is a seasonal item that changes flavor and packaging options a few times during the year. The brand is known as "a brand of the people" for good reason. Another example is AT&T's Business Circle and what they've done on this front with video contests that have videographers seeking out SMBs (small and medium-sized businesses) to profile in order to win a cash prize.[5]

The time you put into your intelligence gathering, going underneath the surface, will determine the depth of your competitive edge and your next best move.

Question 76. Should You Prepare for Social Media as If It Will Hurt Your Brand?

Yes, you should always prepare. You're taking what could turn into a potential negative situation and heading it off by being proactive. Social media can be your greatest source of awareness and engagement or your worst nightmare. Unattended, social media conversations can damage a brand reputation within minutes. You may have seen this happen with Dell "Hell" and Kenneth Cole's #Cairo tweet during the Arab Spring uprisings. When you decide to be actively involved in social communities or if your customers are there talking about you, there is no turning back. The social media floodgates are officially open whether you like it or not. You have to be prepared, and, in the case of Dell and Kenneth Cole, you have to watch what you say or the rate of your response (or lack thereof), respectively.

Setting up your social media presence and sharing information is an invitation for others to learn about you. You can make this a very positive experience. At the same time, you're inviting anyone in your social media communities to be critical of your work. The more you increase the size of your community and your own influence, the more you will hear opinions about what you do, from the good to the bad, and sometimes the very ugly. Negative opinions often have a direct correlation with the size of your network, especially as it increases. Having "haters" just may be a good thing and an opportunity to learn and grow.

Being active in social media always means proactively watching, listening, and making sure you know what is being said about you at all times. It's putting on your social media listening ears, turning up the social media alerts to track your name (check the wrong spelling too) and any topics related to your area of expertise.

Your efforts to watch carefully and to quickly correct what could go wrong are the best way to prevent damage.

Here are three steps to protect your brand as you continue to socialize it:

1. Be proactive and think carefully before you share something. If you get a funny little feeling that hitting the send/share button is not a good idea, then don't do it. Here's a test: How would you feel if it appeared on the front page of *The New York Times* or the *Wall Street Journal*? Or, personally, would what you're sharing pass the family test? Would your mother or grandmother be proud of your communication?
2. Set up alerts or a monitoring system so that you can keep track of what people are saying about you, your company, products, or services. This way you can watch, learn, and steer the

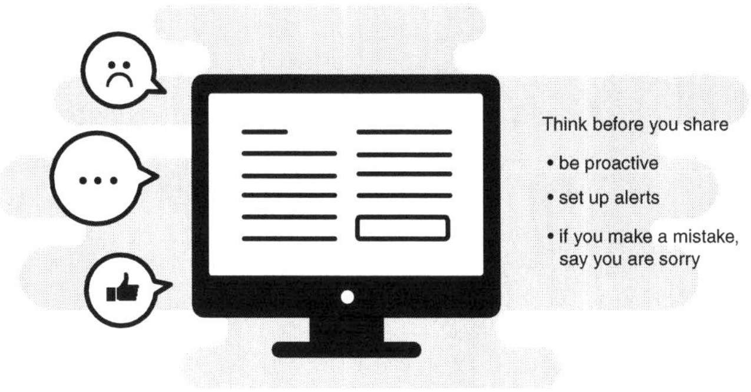

Figure 3.3 Steps to Socialize and Protect Your Brand

conversation in a better direction. Notice I didn't say control ... because we cannot control anything today.

3. If you make a mistake (this is an extension of step 2), say you're sorry. Be accountable for all your actions and do the right thing. Words have consequences, especially on social media. You will neutralize a potentially damaging situation by apologizing and then learning from your mistakes.

If you plan for the negative, as if social media may hurt your brand, then you're ready to handle conversations that could take a turn for the worse.

Question 77. How Can You Travel the World with Social Media?

Social media allows you to work with professionals in other countries. Connecting to areas of the world you could not reach before is not only interesting, but also an amazing learning experience. When it comes to international relationships, there are some important best practices to keep in mind. You have to understand the culture and the customs, as well as how to engage on the accepted platforms.

When I spoke (remotely) to the members of the Iran PR 2.0 Conference in Tehran, a couple of best practices came into play.

First, we agreed on Skype as the preferred business platform for my virtual keynote address.

Second, I quickly researched the Islamic women's dress code and honored their tradition by wearing a light headscarf during my presentation. I wanted to create the best first impression when I "visited" 500 Iranian PR professionals at their annual PR event.

Third, I learned as much as I could about PR in their country from the conference organizer as well as from my own research. I was prepared to deliver a presentation that addressed their needs. PR is different in all different parts of the world, so you have to be sensitive to your audience's needs. At the same time, you'll have a much easier experience during the Q&A if you do your homework.

Social media helps you to make the connection, but then it is up to you to make a good first impression. Make sure you do your homework to explore the different cultures and customs of your international friends. At the same time, when you interact, take the time to listen carefully and really take advantage of what you learn.

Social media allows you to discover so many interesting traditions in exciting and unfamiliar regions of the world.

Question 78. How Do You "Up" Your Learning Online?

Today's classroom has expanded and you can be learning 24/7, if you choose. But, it is up to you to make time for learning. Meeting in the physical classroom will always have tremendous benefits. However, for those who need more flexibility, you can pursue many different options. Online learning has become increasingly popular and a big part of our culture.

Your learning options include everything from online college courses and certificate degrees to social media community learning. You can participate in Twitter chats and LinkedIn Groups. You can also frequent Google+ hangouts and Facebook groups where you can learn from other professionals. If you're a visual learner, then you should check out the video courses on Lynda.com and LinkedIn Learning. I'm a Lynda.com author with several video courses in the areas of PR and marketing.

Of course, you can also take advantage of Massive Open Online Courses (MOOCs), which are a great way to challenge yourself with new areas of interest in the virtual classroom setting. If you decide to explore a marketing and communication MOOC, then you may want to ask the following questions to narrow down your search:

- Have you researched the instructor? What is his/her experience?
- How much will you be able to interact with the instructor?
- Is the course scheduled or self-paced?
- Are you looking for mastery of a topic or general passable knowledge?
- Is the knowledge shared specific to your industry or does it span across different industries?
- Do you understand what is expected from you when you enroll in the course?

If you have the passion and commitment, then you just need to find the time and the best format for you to learn. Education is the key to growth and opportunity. Online or offline, there is a world of new knowledge to discover.

Question 79. Even If You Feel Up to Speed on Social Media, Should You Learn More?

The lesson here is to always learn more. At the start of social media, PR professionals were criticized for not being up to speed on their knowledge and use of social media channels, tools, and tech resources.

I remember participating in a big pitch meeting before social media was mainstream. At the time, blogs were still called "Web Logs." We were trying to secure new business with a tech company that was launching a new load balancer product. We prepared for the pitch and went in sharing all our creative storytelling ideas. We thought we knew the best new ways to reach media and their customers. It was quite a surprise, when we finished sharing our presentation, and the CEO of the company asked, "Where is all of the new media?" *Awkward!*

Here we thought we had pitched the latest media ideas but we missed the mark on blogs, RSS (Really Simple Syndication) feeds and open discussion forums. From that day on, I always made sure we were "up" on our media, whether it was social or otherwise.

As a communicator today, you know that PR and marketing extends far beyond what you were used to or familiar within the "traditional" realm. What you've started to master in the digital PR and marketing arena, and what you've dabbled with on social media, is only the beginning.

There is a new "To Do" list. You will always be checking off activities on this list. But, as soon as you feel like you're up to speed and all caught up, it's time to push the envelope and to learn more.

This is an age of PR and marketing "hustle" and being up to speed is not good enough. When you are not up to speed with the rate of change, you will easily be left behind.

Question 80. How Do You Tap into the Full Potential of Social Media for Yourself?

If you're busy on social media and not excelling in your professional relationships, then you may be doing something wrong. Connecting, chatting occasionally, liking, viewing, and adding a comment here and there is clearly not reaching your full social media or relationship potential.

Now it is time to go deeper. Everything you do for your company or for your clients is what you need to do for yourself. If you understand the concept of community for a business, then what about creating community for you? If you know businesses need influencers and brand champions then what about you—do you need them too? Who are your influencers and how can you create deeper connections with them? If you understand how a business creates awareness and credibility through social media, then what are you doing to increase your own?

To move from communicator in the background and shift all your liaison work to new influential levels, you can use social media to:

- Build your own following, your own friends, fans, and brand advocates; people who will champion for you.
- Create your own influence, but you have to work at it every day; be a helpful resource, take the time to give advice and bring value to your peers. You can take your passion and expertise to new levels.
- Grow your relationships to become reciprocal and leverage them to meet other like-minded influential people.

Treat your own brand like a business and socialize it fully. Now you can tap into the full potential of social media for yourself. Then, when you align your brand with other credible brands, you'll find yourself in really good company.

Question 81. Why Is Social Feedback a Gift?

When someone shares with you, it is a gift. Regardless of the type of comment, he or she took the time to give you some information. This goes both personally and professionally. It's no different for a business; customers are sharing their thoughts all the time. As a rule of thumb, if people take the time to comment, share an idea, or give you feedback, then you need to take even more time to thank them and to respond. Relationships start with simple gestures, courteous behaviors, and showing people that you actually care about what they say. Make it a habit to let people know you appreciate their actions.

There are times when I receive great accolades and then there are those instances when I don't get glowing content reviews. When it comes to sharing content, the more you create and distribute, the more feedback you will receive. However, knowing that a "friend," colleague, peer, or acquaintance wants to give you feedback is an opportunity to listen and learn. When you evaluate the critique, it can help you to figure out how to put your best forward.

I remember after my book *PR 2.0* was published, I participated in a Q&A on an influencer's blog. I didn't feel like I was out of my league, having run an agency for about ten years. The questions were focused on measurement and one of my answers clearly ruffled the feathers of a thought leader in the industry. She slammed my comment and pretty much stated that if I was right then she would eat her shirt (or something to that effect).

At the time, I didn't really know how to answer. So, I didn't respond. I just ignored her comment and hoped it would all go away.

In hindsight, I would have learned a lot if I had politely thanked the influencer and asked for more information about her approach to measurement, and where she might be able to offer more expertise. In the end, I ended up following her closely and I learned so much. Today, I respect and recommend her frequently as an expert.

So the next time you are faced with a comment that looks like it's negative, it's your positive reaction that lets someone know their effort was not wasted. Acknowledging feedback is a great way to show your appreciation and to learn something new at the same time.

Question 82. Should You be the Smartest Person in the Room?

With so much to do every day, you have to use your time wisely. This means using social media to find the greatest thinkers and innovators; those who help you to grow in your career or excel in life because they share valuable information. There is very little to no room for the noise makers in communities, and the "friends" who frequently go on angry rants.

But first you need to figure out what information is critical to your daily function and role; what will help you during the business day and not hinder you. Always look for the people and information that propel you forward, with new ideas or ways to help you tackle challenges. These are the people who know more and have experienced more, and quite often they share a very different perspective.

Once you identify your great thinkers and innovators, you can focus on those inspirational people and learning from them. At the same time, as you discover your true influencers, you will want to do some spring cleaning. You may start by cleaning out your social news feeds (unfollowing or unfriending certain people), opting out of many of the emails that fill up your inbox, and re-evaluating any other unused sources that provide you with a constant flow of information you don't use. Yes, it's time to filter down to exactly what and who helps you to excel vs what and who hold you back.

I have always surrounded myself with great thinkers and innovators who share valuable insights. Remember, what is true for the online realm works offline too. No matter where you are, in order to learn and grow in your career, make sure you are *not* the smartest person in the room.

Question 83. Do You Have a Social Media All-In Reel?

Every year I look forward to International Women's Day. My social media feeds light up with many positive messages and supportive posts from friends, colleagues, and peers. The compliments are plentiful and, as a woman, it feels great to be a part of a nationally recognized day to celebrate women around the world. However, social media is not always supportive and there are negative effects on how you may view yourself just based on the incredible adventures, stories, and news you see posted by your friends.

In a recent interview with Carrie Kerpen, CEO of Likeable Media, on Women Worldwide, she discussed the impact of social media on women. Carrie mentioned the concept of the Highlight Reel, which you see all the time, but may not really verbalize the power of its effects.

The Highlight Reel is the "best of the best" of what a person shares. Now, that's not to say that everything on social media is poised and perfect. After all, Snapchat captures your daily activities in the moment. You have to be quick to "snap" or capture what's going on at any second, unplanned and transparent. But, when you think about the bigger picture, social media has a tendency to showcase the very best moments.[6]

If you're not fully aware, the Highlight Reel can make you feel uncomfortable and uneasy about what you're doing and trying to achieve. Suddenly, when you're looking at all these amazing people in your network, and where they're going and all their incredible opportunities, your life and career may look more challenging or maybe even a little mundane. However, as Carrie points out in her interview, you're not seeing the challenges your friends, colleagues, and peers face in their daily lives. The message Carrie shared was loud and clear. You cannot and should not compare yourself to anyone's Highlight Reel.

How do you combat the Highlight Reel? It's time to start thinking and embracing your own reel. However, perhaps you can call it an "All-In Reel," which is a compilation of the best, the average, and the not so good of what goes on in your world. If you're comfortable in your own skin and you feel you're moving forward in your life and working toward your goals, then looking at someone else's Highlight Reel will not affect you.

The Highlight Reel is not going away. There will always be people in your circles, students in your classes, and professionals in your networks who have amazing stories and adventures. It's time to start working on your own confidence level and how to be secure in what you do. Then, all the comparisons will cease and you'll be sharing not only the best of you but also the real you. Are you All-In?

The Experts Weigh In

Shonali Burke, CEO of Shonali Burke Consulting, Inc.

Design Your Digital Learning Experience

Technology is so all-pervasive in our lives these days. I don't think we are as mindful about it as we could be. But if we take just a few minutes to think about what we want to get out of our careers, we can play a much more active part in our digital learning experience.

I'm not talking about turning our devices off periodically (though that is always good!), or any such initiatives. I'm talking about actually thinking carefully about where we want our careers to go, and the digital skills we need to acquire and hone to get there.

For example, if your sweet spot is content, then are you adept at creating engaging content across a variety of mediums and platforms? Do you know what it takes to socialize this content on a regular basis? Do you know how to build communities around your content?

There are specific techniques and learnings that contribute to each of these. You could stumble upon them—and many of us do!—but you could also approach them in an extremely focused, mindful way.

That's what I mean by designing your digital learning experience in a way that significantly enhances your career.

I recently launched my own online course for the first time, after having taught online for years, at two of the world's most reputed universities. That grounding in navigating online learning environments was invaluable, because I was already comfortable designing and delivering educational instruction online.

But then I had to learn all about email marketing software and systems in a way most PR folk never do. I had to learn how to build a member site. I had to learn all about landing pages, and sales pages, and e-commerce!

It felt really overwhelming—and still does—at times. But all these were specific skills that I learned in order to launch my course. Now, I can also bring these skills to clients who might need them.

Nathan Burgess, Account Supervisor, Digital Strategist, Bliss Integrated

The Next Level of Marketer

The archetypal marketer of tomorrow will be defined by how they're able to blend their own expertise, experience, their client's needs, and the world at large for the benefit of their clients.

There are and have always been good marketers—they are able to sell an idea to the right audience. For "PR pros," that audience has always been the press and that skill is definitely more work and luck than unearned gift.

The next level of marketer is much more business minded—frequently thinking ahead of their client and with one foot rooted firmly in healthy skepticism and the other in enthusiasm. They are always looking forward: What is the story we'll be telling next week? What is the competition working on? What "disruptive" force is going to put us out of business or take us to the next level if we can pivot appropriately?

Over the last several years, we've added a new layer to the cake—technology. When considering social media and "digital" (some ephemeral combination of site content, UX, UI, SEO, and non-social-specific content), the modern marketer has an additional layer of information to assimilate into their client work.

Seeing the whitespace—no matter how new—and filling it in separates the "PR pro" and the "Content person" from the strategist and counselor. Integrating business and the state of the art puts you steps ahead of the game.

These higher-level folks ask, "How can this new technology be put to best use by my client?"

Camera phones, location-based services, drastic cuts in storage and wireless bandwidth costs, at-home broadband penetration, social media, social customer service, and tablet use (already on its way out) presented smart marketers opportunities to be capitalized on or missed.

It's hard to be a first-mover (or second, or third). It's easier to wait for a case study, for all our competitors to claim the space and find where "X" marks the spot. But once they've found the treasure, what is it exactly you'll be looking for?

Ai Zhang, Assistant Professor, Stockton University

A Crisis Moment Resulted in Transformative Changes

One of the compelling issues in public relations education is the disconnect between education and practice. As an educator in this applied field, I have become an adopter and advocate of experiential learning, or learning by doing. A critical element to experiential learning is that educators, *themselves*, are learning by doing. This is especially paramount when it comes to teaching social media-related courses, where ideas and knowledge are being constantly disrupted and (re)invented.

Can PR professors teach social media without being active on and learners of social media? My answer is "No."

In February 2015, I had a profound encounter with one of my PR students who wrote in his paper that he had never heard of Pinterest. That was a wake-up call: I believed that digital natives were digitally savvy, and, clearly, I was being naive. They are not. I saw immediately a gap in my teaching, a disconnect in my classes, and an important missing piece in my students' toolbox—and that gap started with *me* as the educator.

Unless I *practice* what I preach, I will never see the change that I want to see among my students. This realization became the catalyst to embark on a never-ending social media quest. I fully immersed myself into the digital world to learn and build my digital footprint, hoping to lead by example and use my own experience to influence my students. Two platforms that I experimented with heavily are Twitter (especially Twitter Chats) and Snapchat. When I first started this journey, I participated in two to three Twitter Chats a day. I tweeted articles and commented on other people's tweets. I also overcame my fear of videos and dove into Snapchat to tell my stories of being a college professor, a first-generation immigrant, a mother, a wife, and a vegan. I engaged in conversations with people and built relationships with them on a daily basis.

The opportunities I received by creating a visible digital footprint amazed me: Speaking engagements, research collaborations, guest blog invitations, book chapter invitations, and many others. For example, I started a show with a few of my Snapchat friends who are as passionate as I am about digitizing higher education, called "Reimagining Higher Education," where we discuss issues in higher education and best digital practices. I also did two guest blogs that gave me an unbelievable amount of publicity. One is on Brian Fanzo's website, where I discussed how I use Snapchat as a teaching tool, and the other is on Spin Sucks, where I shared how social media transformed my teaching career. My conversation with Brian started via Snapchat, and with Spin Sucks over Twitter. These instances showed me the power of social media in bringing people together to collaborate and initiate change. This human element behind the virtual space is empowering, attractive, and fascinating to me.

In the Chinese language, there are two words used to form the word "crisis": "danger" and "opportunity." A seemingly crisis moment in my teaching resulted in transformative changes and opportunities to my career. As I continue on this journey, I am constantly learning new knowledge and formulating new ideas to embrace and expand the digital me. I am eager to see where and how my career unfolds by following my digital footprint.

Michael Ehrlich (@MichaelEhrlich), Director of Public Relations, Adidas (@adidas)

What it Means to Socialize Your Brand

The days of exclusive daily or long-lead print editorial pieces to tell your story are long gone, so in order to effectively build your brand you *must* socialize it.

In 2017 and beyond, the storytelling landscape will be fully rooted in social media, therefore the opportunities to build your brand are endless. Indeed, this is a huge opportunity to shape your narrative around the clock but, consequently, it comes with a major responsibility, as there is unlimited access and eyes on your brand.

Although my expertise is in the sports world, the lessons I've learned and adopted are applicable to every brand across all industries.

Positioning is everything: Prior to any brand building efforts, you must first take a huge step back and ask yourself a series of questions:

- What does my brand stand for?
- What differentiates my brand across the industry?
- What is my brand's positioning statement?

The thought process and brand soul searching needed to answer these questions will act as a roadmap for building your brand.

No matter the industry, focus, or size, *every* brand must start with a positioning statement. Without one, your communication efforts will be inconsistent and won't make an impact on building your overarching narrative, especially via social media.

Clearly, the positioning statement is the most difficult part of the brand building process, and that's by design. In order to make a splash, you must dive deep into what makes your brand different from your competitors, and determine the *crystal* clear statement that serves as your thread across all communication.

Once you establish your positioning, constancy and frequency are the keys for this statement to stick across the industry, and most importantly with your consumers. Every piece of marketing creative, social copy, and press material must ladder up to your brand positioning. If it doesn't fit, then don't do it.

Fish where the fish are: To socialize your brand, you don't need to be on *every* platform, but the *right* ones, for you.

Carefully select which platforms to launch based on your target consumer, not industry norms or even internal pressures. Fish where the fish are!

Too often, brands choose to create an account on a social channel but don't have the resources, expertise, or brand point of view to activate there effectively. The brand ultimately suffers by socializing where it isn't the best fit.

Just because a new platform is the hot trend across the industry, that doesn't mean your brand has to live there.

Authenticity is key to telling your story, as your target consumers today are more brand-aware than ever before, so it's vital for you and your partners to speak in your own voices when communicating on social media. Anything inauthentic will immediately raise flags with the public and hurt your narrative.

Kids today, especially, are so conscious of their own personal brands on social media that they'll see right through a brand or its partners pushing a corporate message. It's a delicate balance to combine your overarching brand positioning with your target's voice, but it's imperative to socializing your brand.

In addition to your actual social copy, your content on each channel should be unique to the platform. Pushing the same imagery on every social network is never a good look for a brand trying to differentiate itself amongst its competitors. Consumers, media, and industry experts certainly take notice with this lazy approach and it devalues your brand positioning on the most public forum.

Socialize your Own *brand too:* Beyond socializing your employer's brand, communication professionals today *cannot* forget to build their own brand too.

Social is where media break stories, it's where news is driven, it's where brand partners interact with fans, and it *should be* where storytelling professionals live, both to consume and understand media, but also to activate their own narrative and build their personal brand.

Today, having a presence on social media is essential for storytellers. In some instances, social media is even the *best* place to communicate with your media targets, garner coverage, and extend your brand stories.

If you want to be taken seriously as an individual storyteller and power player, build your personal brand on social media.

The social media and storytelling landscape will continue to evolve, so be proactive, take calculated risks and remember that every single message should mirror back to your brand positioning statement.

Good luck!

Notes

1 Brian Solis and Deirdre Breakenridge, *Putting the Public Back in Public Relations* (New York: FT Press, April 2009), 147.
2 Deirdre Breakenridge, *Social Media and Public Relations: Eight New Practices for the PR Professional* (New York: FT Press, April 2012), 37.
3 Suzanne Delzio, Social Media Examiner, "Snapchat Gains Momentum: New Research," February 17, 2016. Available at: www.socialmediaexaminer.com/snapchat-gains-momentum-new-research/ (accessed February 17, 2017).
4 Cotton Delo, *Advertising Age*, "This Brand Hired a 16-Year-Old to Build its Following on Snapchat," January 14, 2016.
5 Steve Olenski, *Forbes*, "Three Global Brands Show How Crowdsourcing is Done," March 28, 2016.
6 Women Worldwide Podcast, "Carrie Kerpen Discusses the Impact Social Media Has on Women," May 30, 2016.

Chapter 4

Taking Your Stories to the Next Level

You should be very familiar with these popular statements: Everyone is a citizen journalist and we're all media publishers today. Social media and mobile technologies make it easier, cheaper, and much quicker for *anyone* to publish content through many different channels. The media landscape is overcrowded and extremely noisy with conversations. People are bombarded with far too many messages, receiving approximately 3,000 to 20,000 per day, ranging from brands they know and like, to many that are considered unwanted disruptions.[1]

I remember reading a *Time Magazine* article quoting information from a Microsoft Corporation study on the human attention span. In 2013, research revealed that humans with a highly digital lifestyle can only pay attention for eight seconds. However, a goldfish—yes, a goldfish—has an attention span of nine seconds. Scary, isn't it? A goldfish can focus longer than one of us.[2]

Where does this leave the modern communicator who is trying to create content for a business that wants to stand out in a very crowded landscape? It takes a different mindset, new methods of research, more creative thinking, advanced tools for content creation, and experimenting with new channels, where you can engage more deeply with your customers and stakeholders. There are big, bold steps necessary to move your stories and your content to the next level. Are you ready to make the move?

I have worked with both large and small brands. My agency's clients have run the gamut from exciting consumer brands to more technical B2B products and services. In both cases, I have experienced content that moves from the so-so, average information to the much more compelling and passion-provoking stories. The questions and answers in this chapter will help you to move into new content creation territories, and really push the storytelling boundaries to build the kind of impact that is critical to your business.

Question 84. How Do You Push Beyond the Familiar Boundaries?

Communicators know the value of earned media, otherwise referred to as the credible third-party endorsement. But, they also realize how the media landscape has changed drastically for consumers. There are new ways to devour information and once-relied-upon channels are oversaturated, delivering thousands of messages. Your customers can easily tune out those brand messages, including yours, if they're not considered relevant at the time. Now, your focus has to expand to different types of media. You have to reach people in many places, opening up the opportunities for you to explore paid, owned, and shared media channels.

By using different types of media, you are more likely to get targeted messages in front of your audience in a way that is easier for them to access. You have to become familiar with a variety of media beyond the earned media you secure. Here are some examples to get you thinking in newer media directions.

Paid Media: Pay-per-click (PPC), display ads, and social media promotions are prime examples of paid media opportunities. Sponsored social media content (i.e., promoted tweets or boosted Facebook posts) and native advertising are also considered paid, too. According to the 2014 Native Advertising Roundup, U.S. spending on native ads is expected to reach $9.4 billion by 2018. From Instagram to Snapchat, communicators are looking for more unique and cost-effective ways to present information, less in the form of an advertisement and more so as a part of their entire media experience.[3]

Shared Media: Shared media comprises your social media channels—Twitter, Facebook, Instagram, LinkedIn, etc. It's where you are distributing content, and your customers are also there commenting, creating, and sharing content through your communities. These opportunities to rally around your stories or the news you share become shared media experiences. Shared media is a great way to interact, offer up subject-matter expertise, and build great relationships, by rallying around good content. At the same time, the people behind the brand are interacting more as peers and less like brands out to market to you and make a sale.

Owned Media: Your owned media can run the gamut from your website copy, blogs, and social media posts to brochures, eBooks, white papers, and your news releases. Owned content lets you tell different types of stories. With more of a timed and developed message you can massage, you're able to share what is top priority and aligned to your higher-level business goals.

When it comes to all your media sharing opportunities, whether you are in a smaller company or a larger one, think PESO (Paid, Earned, Shared, and Owned). At the same time, everyone should work together closely on media initiatives. You have to make it your business to get out of your own department or "silo" to find out what all areas of marketing are doing. The PR, advertising, social media, web, and branding teams must come together for cohesive planning and the better timing of all campaigns. Otherwise, many opportunities to align these areas will be missed. Messages must be consistent throughout all your communication vehicles to keep the brand intact and to prevent fragmentation as you expand through new channels.

If you can stay close to all the marketing communication in your organization, then you can push the boundaries and deliver a mix of media for deeper engagement with your customers.

Question 85. Can You Share a More Visual Story If You Don't Have Deep Pockets?

Visual PR, whether you're using computer generated imagery (CGI), photos, or video, is capturing the attention of audiences worldwide. You can develop your visual toolkit by finding resources in-house, or by aligning yourself with companies that can provide these visual services.

Marketers have always embraced visual and creative design. However, the PR industry really started to embrace Visual PR back in the days of Video News Releases (VNRs) and Multimedia News Releases (MNR). Visuals are one of the best ways to capture and keep audience attention with more interactive and stimulating media. Visual media can tell a powerful story and you don't need deep pockets.

As a modern communicator, you can take a hands-on approach and create interactive content both cost effectively and on the fly. Part of your job is to uncover how audiences like to engage and then build the content that will get their attention. The other part of your job is to identify the right tools and platforms to create your visual

PR, which could be as simple as your own handheld smartphone. Visual storytelling keeps getting better because it is easier for you to create on your own and on the fly.

When I presented a Social Media and PR Tech Testing workshop to a New Jersey group of business owners at a local university, we discussed taking visual stories to new heights. Seizing the moment, I asked if one workshop attendee would participate in an impromptu Facebook Live video interview with me. Out of 25 people, only one business owner raised his hand. I grabbed my phone, stuck it on a travel tripod. Then, I spent about ten minutes with this business owner discussing how social media could help his company. The number of Facebook views and the overall interactions during and after the video proved to be far more engaging than if we had put up a photo of our discussion.

Taking advantage of visual media at my Tech Testing workshop took a minimal amount of time to get the interview live. Of course, had we promoted the FB live weeks in advance, we certainly would have seen a bigger spike in views and my interview guest would have received even more recognition for his company.

Creating a visual story, in this case, was more about changing the mindset of the people at the workshop as opposed to the amount of time or work to set up Facebook Live. Best of all, no creative fees were associated with the effort.

Question 86. Is Anyone Interested in My News?

Chances are, if you develop your company messages and you think they are not exciting, then that is a red flag. You know the difference between a compelling story your customers would find exciting vs one that has no relevance to their lives. In this case, trust your instincts. Why would you share these stories with anyone? Your stories need to capture attention and be truly meaningful. Clearly, it's time to go back to the drawing board.

Remember, when it comes to getting media interest, journalists, bloggers, and busy influencers are subjected to hundreds of pitches and/or messages daily. Your uninteresting pitch will come across as even more mundane. If someone can't make it past the headline or the first paragraph of your email or news release, or any content you send, then the material has very little chance of being published.

You can take the everyday mundane information and reframe it in a different way. Every company has its healthy mix of company announcements, including product launches, new hires, anniversaries, location and space expansions, fundraising efforts, charitable giving, revenue growth, new business development, customer success stories, etc. However, to increase your coverage, every time you want to share, ask yourself if your news meets one of the four "Cs" to entice the media to write about your stories:

1. *Current events* and using research to tap into what is relevant in the news. Research can be obtained from surveying brands/companies, industry groups, and your customers that have not been previously shared publicly. You can also monitor social media conversations and trending topics to see what's trending globally, or how you can tap into stories of regional or local interest.
2. *Commentary* from your respected thought leaders who can speak with authority on timely news topics that affect your industry, the market landscape and your customers. The more you can get their perspective and insights to the media when they need input, the more you become a valuable resource and trusted source over time.
3. *Controversy,* which always makes the news, gets attention. You may be able to offer a contrary view to a popular topic or share your thoughts on a controversial industry matter. Just being a part of the discussion and taking a different or unique stance can raise your brand profile.
4. *Caring stories* or news that is tied to human interest. If what you do is tied to or affects the health and well-being of others, then by all means highlight and share the stories of different groups to join the discussion and to highlight the triumphs of others.

Question 87. How Can My Company be a Media Publisher Today?

Today every person can be a publisher and so can every company. The saying, "every company is a media company," was coined by Tom Foremski, who was the first journalist to leave a major newspaper to blog. His saying caught on rather quickly. You may be used to telling stories and you probably know the value of good storytelling. However, these stories were disseminated through one-way channels and were focused on a company's news and messaging,

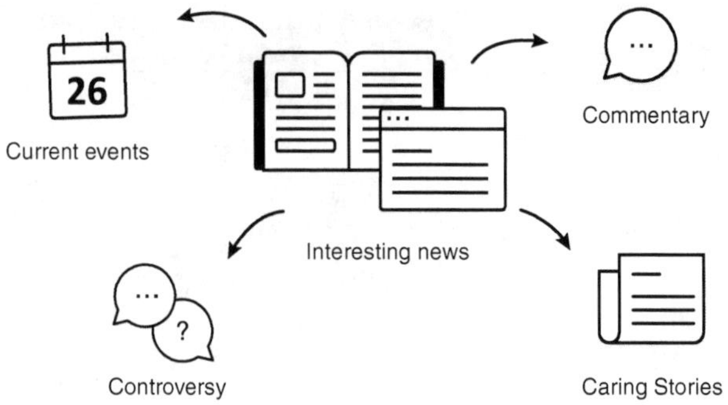

Figure 4.1 The 4Cs of Interesting News

whether it was regarding the company's customers, employees, growth or partnerships, etc.

Today, storytelling takes a different form. Companies are still reporting on their own news, but they're also hiring journalists, bloggers, and outside storytellers to create content for them. The stories take a different approach, as they are written solely to help their customers, or report on interesting subjects outside of their own self-promotion. The company is no longer the focal point of every story; it doesn't have to be. Great examples that come to mind are American Express with Open Forum and GM with A Taste of General Mills.

PR is naturally poised to play a part of the storytelling process and the publishing of content beyond company announcements. If you're a communicator, then you're not only a storyteller, but you are also working with your organization to be a media publisher and incorporate brand journalism into what you share.

Question 88. How Do You Create a Media Hub?

Years ago, we saw the rise of the cyber or online newsroom; a place where media would go to access important information about your business, executives, company vision and mission, FAQs, product information, presentations, news releases, images, etc. The newsroom housed everything journalists needed to access to build and enhance their stories. In addition, the newsroom also offered journalists the opportunity to find the PR contact information to easily reach out for more information, or to request a subject-matter expert (SME) interview.

Today, the newsroom goes beyond the journalist and is now a media center or hub. The media hub moves beyond your company news and creates a full repository of information, allowing easy access to materials beyond what journalists or bloggers need. Media hubs are content centers set up for all company stakeholders, including employees, shareholders, partners, vendors, and customers. A repository of information should be available and updated 24/7 with all different types of content that tells the brand's stories.

If you have yesterday's newsroom on your company website, then it is time to morph this area into today's media center so you can share updated information regularly. By sharing all content about your company you're assisting more people when they need information.

Your goal is to welcome and provide relevant material to all your stakeholders when they reach out for help.

Question 89. Why Is It Important for Your Employee Culture to Tell the Story?

Culture is engrained in your business. It lives, breathes and grows through your employees. Once rooted in your organization, your employees speak the language of the company culture as your brand champions; living the brand at work and after hours. Culture is what makes great companies stand out and what makes people want to be a part of your organization, whether that translates into working as an employee or becoming a loyal customer.

When your culture permeates beyond your own four walls that means:

1. Employees are actively sharing their own company experiences.
2. Employees are telling the story about the business for you.
3. Employees tell your story, which gets more recognition from their networks of friends and peers.
4. People will appreciate employee communication much more than any prose crafted by your communications team.

Your role is to help draw out those outstanding stories, interactions, and involvement from within. Always encourage employees from different departments to share their best experiences as proud members of your company.

Figure 4.2 When Culture Permeates Your Own Four Walls

The strength of your culture will always shine through more when employees do the storytelling for you.

Question 90. What Does It Mean to be a Content Machine?

A content machine is a fine-tuned and well-oiled engine that creates, distributes, and measures the performance of content using the most efficient process. Before you can even think about specific content and steady distribution, you have to get your content engine into place.

There are simple steps to get your content workflow flowing:

1. Evaluate your current internal platform/sharing resources and content development process for social media sharing.
2. Decide what works and update your process to meet your expected social media sharing needs, keeping in mind resources to keep your engine fine-tuned over time.
3. Set up an updated workflow process taking the best of what you do forward with a few different roles to make social media sharing easier and more productive.
4. Assign team members specific roles. Ask who will be on the creative strategy and brainstorming team? Who will design the content and approve the creative? Who will be the content creators (the contributors) vs the editors for approval? Who will manage the process on a regular basis and be the internal liaison to make your process flow? Who will distribute the content through your channels and analyze the performance analytics?

5. Designate a community manager to take the role of storytelling champion who is also present and watching, interacting, and fielding questions about your content.
6. Use your engagement and content performance analytics as a guide for generating new content through your new workflow process.

Even the smallest companies can put this type of process into place (just on a smaller scale). If you get into the habit of a routine content development and sharing process, then you can start small and ramp up as more resources become available. As you do, you will see more performance around your content in the form of deeper engagement with happy customers.

Question 91. What's the Best Way to Manage Content and "Urgent" Conversations?

The community manager plays a very important role for your company. If this is your role, then you are the face of the company on social media; a great host and storyteller, a brand champion, and the "connector" between the brand and the people. As the community manager, the more you share content, the more active you will be in guiding conversations and answering questions. At some point, you may even question what are the most urgent conversations to address?

Corina Manea, Chief Community Officer at Arment Dietrich & Spin Sucks and Founder of NutsPR, discovered that no matter how urgent some things are, you need to stop and take a step back. If you do, then you can identify and listen to your audience, the very same people with whom you want to share your content. Here are Corina's four steps to managing the flow of content and community engagement:

1. Whether the brand is just starting out on social media or already established, defining the audience is the first step before creating and sharing content.
2. After identifying the audience, find members on their favorite social media channels and *"listen"* to them: What they like or dislike, what they share, or talk about, where else they hang out.
3. Armed with this information, it comes naturally to create and share content for clients' social media channels for those specific

audiences. People want to be listened to by the brands they like and follow.

4. Another way to make a difference is to directly interact with a client's audience. Simple things such as "how are you," and "we like your content," helped start the conversation and, further, led to finding out what they expected from the company in terms of content they wanted to see, and products or services they wanted to buy.

Corina says, "The secret is not so secret. Making a difference in social media is to be human and care about those people you're trying to reach." She stresses how you should connect with community members as humans, not as a brand trying to sell something. If you do, you will be amazed by the results: ambassadors for your brand and customers interested in your company's products and services.

Regardless of your size, having the people, process, and technology in place first will really help you to manage the conversations, but, more importantly, the human interactions that lead to great relationships.

Question 92. How Do You Share Meaningful Information When You Have Writer's Block?

If you have ever experienced writer's block, then you know it can be frustrating, especially if your job is solely focused on writing or even just in part. In either case, here are a few tips to combat writer's block, so you can get your creative and business writing back on track.

1. The first step is to clear your mind. Doing a brain dump of all the tasks you have to do, or removing from your mind anything personally or professionally weighing you down, truly helps to raise your creative energy. Really clearing your mind can open up your thought process so you can start writing again.
2. Next, don't think about a perfect completed piece. Rather, just do a stream of conscious on a topic you like. Sometimes, I just do my own little brainstorm on a white board, or you can do this in your favorite note-taking software. I use Evernote when I want to capture my thoughts using voice command. The outcome is nowhere near a finished product, just phrases and thoughts that come to mind. Doing this solo exercise allows you

to see the potential of the topic and visualize how you can take your thoughts further in a more structured manner.

3. Lastly, for me, the mini staycation gets my writing back on track. Sure, I would love to book a trip to an island or European getaway every time I feel bogged down, which deters me from my writing. However, it is not realistic. But a little mini staycation, at home, is the perfect way to take a morning, an afternoon, or even a whole day to rejuvenate. My staycation means taking time to do things as if I am on vacation … morning meditation, bicycle riding, massage therapy, swimming, and some shoe shopping.

By the time I'm done with my mini staycation, the block is gone and I'm ready to write again.

Question 93. Should I Focus More on Digital or My Traditional Communication Strengths?

Always take the best of the past forward with you. I started in PR with news release and media pitch writing. Eventually, I advanced to byline articles, editorial opinion pieces, newsletter copy, website, and brochures. After about ten plus years, I added to my repertoire executive communication, including interview talking points, speeches, and annual reports.

The writing, earlier in my career, didn't necessarily prepare me for some of the social media writing on different channels today. How could it? The media world has changed. For example, I launched my PR Expanded blog (formerly called PR 2.0) back in 2007 to find out quickly that the writing was much more informal and conversational than what I was used to when I first started out in PR. I remember a blogger friend of mine giving me some good advice. He said, "Deirdre, you really have to work on your 'raw'." I knew exactly what he meant. Cue the human and personal side of blog writing; no trained media spokesperson rhetoric allowed.

From that point forward, I quickly learned the difference between blogging and other writing styles. I also mastered writing status updates for Twitter, Facebook, and LinkedIn, always focusing on what my audience preferred to hear about or learn from me.

Good writing is essential in PR. Of course, you still need to master the more "traditional" types of writing. However, it is also time to roll up your sleeves for social media writing, especially as new channels continue to proliferate. Learning different styles of writing will not only add to your skills portfolio, but also really play up your digital strengths.

Here's a quick checklist of new media storytelling that you should navigate with ease:

- blogs
- video scripting
- social networks
- micromedia
- infographics
- tip sheets
- eBooks
- microsite content.

Of course, the list is not comprehensive, it's only a small snapshot. But, it incorporates enough of the new storytelling areas; the channels communicators should feel comfortable writing for and places where their customers congregate. Remember, types of media will change, but your ability to be a good writer and storyteller will be a constant.

Question 94. How Do You Craft Eye-catching Headlines?

The best headlines are eye-catching. Let's start with the media and the headline of your news releases or your pitches, which are key factors in securing editorial placements. If the headline is not interesting to the journalist or blogger, then there is no need to read the body of the release or your pitch letter. Many journalists believe the best headlines imply the advice, education, or groundbreaking information they will find in the body of your story.

However, eye-catching headlines go well beyond the news release and your pitch. Think about headlines in all your writing. Your email subject lines, the title of articles you post on your blog, the names of your YouTube videos, and the titles for your eBooks and infographics. All these "headlines" are important to grab your readers' attention. If you can't grab them at "hello," then what you create in the body of your work will not get the attention it deserves.

Think about why you open emails that land in your email inbox, read magazine articles online, and watch and share your favorite videos. How important is the headline or title in determining the time you invest in reading news and information? I remember reaching out to a local business publication that shared its daily newsletter capturing the day's headlines. Instead of enticing me to open the email newsletter with a great subject-line, the publication would put the same thing in the headline each day. They would use the name of the publication along with the company who sponsored the issue. Although this may be great for their sponsors, this did nothing for me. With a number of more preferred publications showing up in my inbox, this newsletter was deleted more often than not. Finally, I just hit that little link to unsubscribe.

The best practice here is to use your own attention span and preferences to guide you. Use your own personal test to help you create eye-catching headlines for your customers and the people who need to hear from you.

Question 95. Should You Still Write and Distribute Good News Releases?

When it comes to good news release writing, the optimal word here is "good." A news release is still an opportunity to share a well-written, timely news story your audience wants or needs to know.

When you write news releases for your company, you should avoid emotional phrases, sales language, and opinions. In my experience, I've worked with executives who often want to "enhance" the language in the release depending on the type of news. You can gently explain that some stories are better shared through other more appropriate channels. For example, your news release should capture the hard-hitting newsworthy facts and information in an impartial and unbiased manner. You can always take the emotional appeals, creative writing, and more inspirational articles and package them for your blogs or other social media communities for your stakeholders. Videos are also a great way to tell a human and emotional story that tugs at the heartstrings. The good news is the enhanced story will not be lost. You'll be able to customize your story and find it a home through social media.

When you want to share a news release, think beyond the journalist to the people he/she is sharing the news with. The key is to give the media what they need for their communities. After all, if your journalist friends are supposed to report the news, then you need to help them do just that … offer newsworthy information in a format that helps them to build their stories.

And, just for the record, if media professionals, and other groups are finding, reviewing, and using good news releases, then you should keep writing and sharing them. Regardless of the format of the release which is much more interactive and visual, or where you post them, a good story will get good coverage.

Question 96. How Do You Know What to Share on Social Media?

You don't have to wrack your brains about what content is the most important to share for your audience. Too many times, professionals in the boardroom discuss content for their customers without even stopping to think about what those customers really want or need. Why don't you just ask them?

Social media makes it unbelievably easy to find out what people like and what gets them into a sharing mood. You don't have to guess any more. Here are three simple steps to find out quickly what people really want from you.

1. You can monitor conversations to see what issues or questions pop up. Even better, you can take the time to ask your community on Facebook or on Twitter. When you inquire, people are more than happy to share. Of course, then you need to be there to guide the conversation and to build ideas together, if they want your help.
2. Another great way to learn about the content your customers prefer is to analyze the content on your website. If people are spending time reading your blogs, watching your videos, or reviewing new product pages, then you're doing something right. Your web analytics (we use Google Analytics) will tell you exactly what people are doing and how long they stay on your website pages. When you can determine content and the information that garners the most time and interest, you can use that information to fuel your content sharing moving forward.
3. You can learn what people are doing the most in your social media communities. A social media content audit is a great way to get a snapshot of sharing levels, based on content interest. If you can determine the types of content people like, share more, or comment on the most, then you will want to create more of what they like to satisfy their needs and their content appetite.

Learn by listening, asking, or analyzing what people prefer. When you do, your customers will appreciate you and your content much more, as they are consulted and considered as a part of the creation process.

Question 97. How Can You Make It Easier for People to Find Your Content?

About ten plus years ago, many PR people didn't think or even care about search engine optimization (SEO). Personally, I used to think it was someone else's job. At my agency, when SEO was needed for a client, it was an area handled by the digital marketing and our web teams. Initially, I thought SEO *only* meant the use of Meta Tags embedded in your website. Then, when consumers searched for certain keywords, they would see your company come up in the Search Engine Result Pages (SERPs).

Of course, as I worked more closely with my agency's marketing team, I learned how adding metadata including keywords, tags, and meta descriptions to your content, and everything you post, increased your visibility considerably. Today in PR, you are creating just as much content as the marketing and the web teams. As a matter of fact, all the content you create needs to be picked up by the search engines when your customers and other important constituents search.

You have to make sure your content is found. Every photo, image, video, and piece of content must also be optimized for the search engines. After all, why build it if no one can find it? Make it easy for your audiences by optimizing your content and they will find you on their own. Other important SEO considerations include:

1. Always create great content that is relevant to your audience.
2. Keep your content fresh and update your website frequently.
3. Optimize your content titles and descriptions, making them more interesting and readable.
4. Use location-specific keywords or localize your content so local audiences can find you.
5. Build your social media content and your social profiles, as these pages are appearing higher in the search engine results.

If there was any doubt before, now you know—SEO is a part of the modern communicator's role.

Question 98. Can You "Control" Your Stories After They Are Shared?

You spend time carefully crafting stories for different audiences. However, once your story is shared publicly, you lose all control over how it will be perceived and how opinions are formed. Most of all, you can't control what will be said about you. Then, add social media into your communications and your story can change even more quickly. You are giving people the opportunity to take what you say and actively add their own personal touch. They're creating content based on what they perceive from your original messages, regardless of whether it is in a positive or negative light.

Wherever you communicate, through any number of channels, there is no guarantee that your original story or messages will remain intact. For this reason, I have learned the importance of not only tracking what is being said based on what I share, but also building strong relationships in my communities with people who will support me when I need them. Building relationships with the right influential people, whether they're members of the media, bloggers, or other well-known and credible personalities, will help to propagate the positive messages and champion your communication.

Do you remember the #McDStories hashtag? McDonalds thought their customers would hear about the campaign and share their favorite, heartwarming McDonald's stories. Instead, they got a lot of #McDStories that were a complete #Fail and the campaign moved from hashtag to "bashtag." People told stories related to their weight gain and the times McDonald's made them sick to their stomachs. They used the hashtag and the campaign certainly got a lot of recognition, but for all the wrong reasons. McDonald's couldn't control their message, which went in a completely different direction. However, they were on top of the negative stories and quickly acted to "fix" the situation.[4]

You may never be able to control again. But, you can certainly put your resources in the right places to guide the conversations and to get your communication back on track.

Question 99. How Can Data Help My Communication?

Today, the words "big data" are everywhere, from the Mashable and TechCrunch articles to the new conferences and events popping up worldwide. How can a modern communicator take big data and use it as smart data in a communications program?

First, you have to understand that big data is useless without proper filtering and the right analysis to turn your information into actionable insights. You can pull all the data you want, but if it is not accurate (free from "spammy" information) and if it is not examined critically, then you will have an over-abundance of useless data.

At the same time, you have to do your homework by researching and selecting the tools that give you the flexibility you need to capture good data. For example, do you require a tool that collects data across a large community or across several communities? Do you need a resource that gives you sentiment analysis to determine if the conversations you are collecting are positive, negative, or neutral? Or, do you want tools that are free vs paid due to budgetary constraints? These are all important items to evaluate when you're embarking on big data and using the information you glean to make a decision.

Of course, you wouldn't be capturing data if you didn't know exactly what you were trying to achieve. Are you using the data to better understand the market landscape and your competition, or to learn more about your customers? Perhaps, the data will help you to optimize your marketing programs? Will data help you to make a more creative media pitch? Or, maybe listening closely to your audiences will reveal new product ideas and enhancements or ways to innovate together. There are many strategic uses of the data, but knowing why and how you want to use your data will produce better results.

Most of all, don't try to tackle too much data at once, because it can be paralyzing. An over-abundance of data can lead to information overload and data paralysis. Instead, you can start bigger and then filter down to smaller sets of data. Ultimately, this process will lead to those smarter actionable insights for your business or your communications programs. In the end, you'll find the smaller data sets give you the big direction you will need to move forward with confidence.

The discussion about data will continue for many years to come. Data is the future of communications. Whether we call it big data or smart data, it is here to stay. When modern communicators understand the value and roll up their sleeves to experience data first hand, then they too will be proving their data literacy and using smart data for better communication.

Question 100. How Do I Jumpstart a Brand Journalism Program?

Brand journalism is more than just a buzzword; it has real value for the brands telling their stories in a journalistic way through different types of media. The stories are shared in a style that engages their customers and stakeholders; similar to how their favorite media properties would interest them.

With brand journalism, your sharing will go beyond your own news and will be more focused on informing your audience about important trends and developments in your market, regardless of whether these situations involve your own company. The focus of the story is on the audience; the way good reporting or storytelling should be.

If you are thinking of jumpstarting your brand journalism program, here's how to approach your owned content:

1. Think like a reporter and not a marketer. Your products and services take a back seat and you are sharing information that impacts your community's perceptions.
2. Stay focused on your outcome and not the marketing funnel for a sale. You should be delivering information that is relevant and meaningful to your audience, similar to a media outlet.
3. Use a variety of content and keep it housed in a central hub. You want to draw people in with good content so they will want to spend time on your website to learn more. If you draw them into your newsroom, media center, or blog, then give them a reason to stay.

Brand journalism is a way to create owned content that has a broader appeal to people who want far more than just your company news and product information.

Question 101. How Are Content and Influencer Marketing Related?

Content marketing should be not only on your radar, but also a part of your communication planning. Yes, we're all content marketers today. Of course, whether you consider yourself a marketer or a PR person, you need to come up with a good plan for your content. Your plan should focus on how you will create and share the most relevant content to raise awareness, create thought leadership, or drive engagement that results in leads and sales for your products.

Content is an opportunity to have people rally around important information. Of course, finding the right people who drive community conversations (the influencers) is the best way to make your content go the distance. As trusted sources in their communities, influencers naturally increase awareness, interactions, and overall action.

As a content marketer, it is your job to find these influencers and to understand when and how they share. Here's one way to categorize your influencers and to tap into their sharing habits. Your influencers can be broken down into five behaviors:

1. *Simple Sharer:* Happy to like, retweet, and share any piece of content on your behalf.
2. *Amplifier:* Goes to greater lengths to share your content across different social media communities.
3. *Social Connector:* Beyond the Amplifier, the Social Connector takes your content, writes about it, and then targets and connects other people to your content.
4. *Cheerleader:* These are special influencers because they know how to rally the crowd. They are the motivators and people pleasers.
5. *Reviewer/Endorser:* Reviews and critiques your products and services on a deeper level. The Reviewer and Endorser are willing to put a stamp of approval on your brand.

Going back to the days of E. F. Hutton, which was an American Stock Brokerage Firm, I remember how their campaign touted, "When E. F. Hutton talks people listen." Similar to influencers in your social communities today, not only do people talk and their peers listen, but they also are more likely to take action.

Figure 4.3 The Five Behaviors of Influencers

The best part of working with influencers ... at the intersection of content and influencer marketing is community member action!

Question 102. Should You Develop Your Content in Real Time?

Stories develop over time and in real time. As a storyteller, sometimes the research is in-depth and the writing process longer. At other times, you can let the details unfold as they occur. The latter is the nature of social media and real-time news. Chances are you have a storytelling device in your hand right now, or one that is less than three feet away from your body. Yes, your smartphone has the ability to create quick streaming video and to create and share photos in an instant.

Of course, you will always be creating the longer-form types of content that take time and require careful planning. But, don't forget that you can capture important moments, or a snapshot in time. Perhaps these moments create momentum and offer a behind-the-scenes experience. People are consuming information in real time, so your stories have to meet the needs of their media consumption habits.

One famous example that sticks in my mind ... Oreo cookies and their real-time advertisement after the lights went out during the Super Bowl in 2013. The ad tagline was "You Can Still Dunk in the Dark." This is one of many uses of real-time content marketing, with exposure that captured attention at the right moment, and, as a result, was shared virally.

Another great impromptu marketing example is when Arby's seized an opportunity to tweet about Pharrell Williams at the 2014 Grammy Awards program. Pharrell wore a hat that night that looked like the Arby's logo. They tweeted to @Pharrell with the #Grammys hashtag, opening up their tweet to anyone watching the Grammys and using the hashtag. One humorous tweet led to over 81,000 retweets. But, the real marketing opportunity occurred when Pharrell auctioned the same hat to raise money for a charity to help children. Arby's very smartly bought the hat for over $41,000.00. What a great real-time PR and marketing story!

Real-time marketing is not planned and you can't just plug it into your storytelling and content strategy. You just don't know when it is going to happen. However, your ability to be there, listening, participating, and being flexible with your content sharing are the secret ingredients to a real-time marketing recipe.

Question 103. Can You Raise Your Own Thought Leadership Through Storytelling?

PR professionals used to be the liaisons behind the scenes. We were the managers and the coordinators. Although we still serve an important liaison role, social media has elevated our ability to become PR 2.0 champions. We can take our own education, thought leadership, and storytelling to the next level. Being active on social media, networking, and collaborating with colleagues and sharing your insights in your communities is a great way to be a go-to-resource. When you share valuable information on social media, you raise your credibility.

Sharing great information is nothing new. I've always been a proponent of writing for PR or marketing publications, which gives you more credibility as an expert in your field. If you write a column for PRWeek or Adweek, or you're asked to contribute content to any of the well-known marketing blogs, then you have a platform to share and become an expert voice. Researching topics and writing is a wonderful way to keep your eyes and ears close to your industry, keeping you abreast of the latest trends.

At the same time, your writing is an opportunity to be recognized by your industry and peers, which can raise your profile and lead to more thought leadership opportunities.

Your credibility is directly related to how much you participate as an expert in your field. Contributing content is one of the best ways to raise the bar and to raise your credibility at the same time.

The good news ... sure you can write for industry publications or you can take your expertise to other valuable channels. For example, look at the many YouTubers who have amassed millions of followers and the lifestyle bloggers who are valued for their tips and insights. Today, whether you choose to be a blogger, a podcaster, a digital correspondent, or a magazine contributor, you can move from the background into the foreground. It's time to build your own community and be a valuable resource.

Question 104. How Do You Ignite Your Internal Champions and Get Them to Write?

You can't just expect employees to be your brand champions. You can't tell them to be champions either. You have to build champions starting from the inside of your company. In order to "live the brand," you have to first understand and believe in the brand. Many companies will partially share information with employees. In turn, they expect them to share the news announcements or marketing campaigns with their family and friends.

If you want people to write and share on your behalf, whether it is for you personally or for a business, you have to involve them and make them feel a part of your brand. People have to be excited about what they do, how they are involved, and where the brand is headed. They won't just share for the sake of sharing. You have to ignite their passion and create a deeper emotional connection. The level of the understanding and connection to the brand is directly proportionate to the level of sharing.

Here are four ways to get your champions on board and sharing for you.

1. *Survey your employee base to gauge their level of understanding and use of social media:* Surveys are a great way to let your champions stand out when they answer questions about their personal social preferences (especially when you have open-ended questions). You'll quickly find out what employees want to learn with respect to sharing on social media for the company.
2. *Conduct informal in-depth interviews with potential champions who stand out in your company:* Look beyond marketing to your customer service, sales, HR, IT, and other departments—people happy to share their thoughts about their own social involvement, conversations, and engagement. Many employees will offer ideas and opinions on what your company could be doing and how they can help.
3. *Use a social media platform for good communication within your own four walls:* You can invite people to share, collaborate, and innovate together on an internal social media platform. These platforms are designed for brainstorming, real-time discussion, and document sharing, etc. When people come together there is synergy and learning.
4. *Recognize or incentivize your employees to get them social for you:* There are internal sharing platforms that help companies create healthy competition among employees who share approved social media messages. The more they share the company stories, the more they are recognized or rewarded. These rewards can include anything from nominal gift certificates to lunch with an executive of the company.

After all, you know the saying … sharing is caring.

Question 105. Should I Take My Stories to Newer Channels?

For all modern communicators, it is your job to understand where you need to engage if you want to build deeper relationships. Of course, this always depends on your customers and the constituents you're trying to reach, and on where they prefer to congregate on social media.

Here's where being a Tech Tester really pays off. If you're a Tech Tester, then you are the professional who is always exploring technology and learning how and why audiences participate in different social communities. For example, the Tech Tester knows that it is his or her job to be ten steps ahead of their customers. It is one thing to know about a platform, but it is another to research, explore, and actually use the functionality.

For those companies who have an audience that skews younger, then you have a reason to be on Snapchat. Some companies have given the reins of their accounts to younger bloggers to rack up on new members. At the same time, younger staff members who are personally familiar can help to manage your account. Of course, if you are a brand with an older demographic, then you should still keep your eyes on Snapchat. The age group is slowly expanding to the 35+ category.

For me, I'm not super active on Snapchat, but I've set up my account to get a good feel for the different ways to share from snaps, to stories, to how you can interact with many different brands. Many of my favorite news outlets are on Snapchat. Of course, marketers should also pay close attention to the advertising on this platform. Then, when you're CEO or senior-level executive say, "Should we be on Snapchat and would this make sense for brand awareness?" You will know the answer and be able to say why or why not.

The same goes for any new platform; it may be Snapchat and Facebook Live today, but who knows what new "shiny" platforms will be available tomorrow. Where the news is shared, where the people go, and where you are talked about are certainly reason to explore and quite possibly take your storytelling to these new channels.

Question 106. How Can Influencers Help Your Storytelling?

Influencers can help to amplify your stories and spark their communities into action. But, first you have to work really hard to build relationships with them. I start with understanding the types of influencers based on their network participation and how they share. When you categorize your influencers it allows you to see more about their interactions with their community members, the extent of their sharing and who they are attracting in their communities. With so many influencers, you need to put your time and energy into building the right relationships.

As you start out identifying your influencers, you can also categorize them by their followers and the ways you think they may want to participate in your programs.

1. *A-Listers:* These influencers compare to a top tier publication such as *The New York Times* or the *Wall Street Journal*. Bloggers who are A-List look for the groundbreaking and novel stories. They have very large networks and their interest in your story is a big driver of awareness and traffic to your website.
2. *Trendsetters:* These influencers are very passionate about a specific topic or industry. They choose to follow a company or a story from start to finish. Although their followers are considerably less than the A-List influencers, their passion for a subject is just as big. Unlike the A-List, these influencers want you to reach out when there are changes at your company. They remind me of trade journalists who are very targeted in their reporting.
3. *Up and Comers:* These are the influencers who are on their way up the ladder. They have smaller networks but aspire to be Trendsetters or A-List Influencers. When you build a relationship with an Up and Comer you will end up growing together. They will be more likely to take you to the top with them—if you prove to be a good, reliable, and trusted source. Many companies forget to take advantage of the Up and Comers, often opting for more exposure rather than a growing relationship.
4. *The Magic Middle:* There's definitely magic at this level of a social media community. It is the area where most communicators (or companies) are not invited. The level of interaction is deeper and the relationships forged are very close knit. Think about mommy bloggers who are really close to their communities. When they speak, other mommies listen and even purchase products they share. Working with influencers who command the Magic Middle is an invitation to reach the people who will not only want to know about your product but who'll also be more likely to make a purchase.[5]

5. *Your own employees:* There is one group you should never neglect: your own internal champions, who you can motivate to share with their friends and families. However, you can't just tell your employees to be your influencers and your champions. On the contrary, you have to educate and include them in your brand building and storytelling. You have to make them feel a part of the company progress and they'll share your stories long after the workday ends.

Influencers come in all shapes and sizes. I would rather have ten close relationships than a list of hundreds of influencers who probably don't care about what my company does or what my clients care about. Building relationships will always be hard work and there are no short cuts. But, once you've gained the interest and a mutually beneficial relationship, the storytelling is propelled to a whole new level.

Question 107. What Does It Take to Start a Podcast?

Just like any type of media distribution, podcasting requires careful consideration. But, is podcasting right for everyone? Will you capture your audience's attention so that they become your loyal podcast fans? There are several factors to consider before your dive into podcasting, especially when you know every media initiative takes precious time and resources.

Here are five tips to help you if you're interested in launching a podcast and creating a devoted community of listeners.

1. *Know your purpose:* Ask yourself, "What is my passion and what am I trying to achieve?" You should select a show theme that you love in order to commit the time and energy necessary to make your podcast a long-term success. Of course, nailing down what success looks like is a critical first step. Goals and objectives should be specific. Are you trying to reach your base or perhaps increase your community size? Do you want to monetize your podcast (how much; by when)? Are you interested in creating a network that goes beyond your podcast show? Are you trying to educate listeners and use your podcast as a thought leadership platform? Drilling down the details and benchmarking over time will help you to stay on track and reach your intended goals.

2. *Talk to other podcasters:* When you talk to people who are already podcasting or those working with podcasters on the production side, it really helps you to understand the time, energy, and resources needed for your own program. Before I decided to dive into podcasting, I spoke with several podcasters to find out how they readied their content for primetime. I also formed alliances with strong partners who could do the heavy lifting when it came to producing, distributing, and promoting my show.
3. *Spread the word about your show, everywhere you go:* You have to let everyone know that you are podcasting. From your networking and speaking events to your website and social media communities, get excited and "talk up" your show. Whenever I share information about Women Worldwide, the outcome varies. These outcomes include friends and colleagues sharing show ideas and topics, being introduced to amazing guests, sponsors, and advertisers who become interested, and my community growing with more listeners.
4. *Measure success with numbers:* Podcast measurement is easy because you can go by the numbers. We use Libsyn Hosting to gauge which shows create the most interest by the number of downloads. We are able to identify where the download numbers are coming from; whether it is a marketing campaign through mobile ads or via Facebook. At the same time, we can review listener demographics including country, state, city, and the gender of our listeners.
5. *Listen to feedback and grow:* Feedback is a gift whether it is positive or negative. I've learned from my listener feedback to laugh and be more relaxed, share personal stories, and interview guests who have experienced challenges on their way to success. Feedback is the only way you will learn and grow. Plus, if you incorporate listener feedback into your show, your community knows you care and you value their opinions.

Question 108. Should My Executives be on Social Media Telling Stories?

It depends on the executives. Some executives have a knack for technology and social collaboration. I remember speaking at a media relations conference in Palm Springs. Speaking on my panel was the president of a university who was one of the most active members in higher education at the time. He used Twitter as a way to get closer to his students, their parents, and other higher education constituents. He was a stellar example of a leader on social media.

Then there are other cases. There are executives who want to be on social media but just don't have the time. They start a Twitter account, begin blogging, and set up their LinkedIn profiles. The issue with these busy executives is what they start, they can't finish, based on the nature of their positions and demands during their days (and nights). When you have an eager but busy executive with a hectic schedule, it is best to capture their image or their thought leadership. Then you can share what they say through the company's official social media feeds. They may not be tweeting but they still have a presence and are best representing the organization.

Of course, there are those executives who think they can do and say anything on social media. Your best bet here is to get them some good social media training or, as a last case scenario, take away their smartphones. Tweetstorms at 3:00 a.m. are generally not a good idea. Of course, if any executive has the passion to communicate and has a good handle on what it takes to contribute valuable information or be a helpful resource, then, by all means, this is an executive gift that should be cultivated.

Here are a few questions you can ask yourself before you give your executives the keys to host your social media profiles:

1. What is your executive trying to achieve by using social media?
2. Will your executive be able to communicate with authenticity and transparency (polished imagery does not work)?
3. Is your executive briefed on your social media policy (and do you have one)?
4. Will your executive be able to keep up with the social media conversations? You can't start a conversation and then jump ship if people have questions.
5. What platforms does your executive feel most comfortable using and has he or she had any training?

There are plenty of reasons for executives to take to social media to embrace authentic conversations and to build stronger relationships. I find that many of the executives that excel on social media are actually better listeners than they are communicators. They have their big listening ears on and they're in communities to help, guide, and always give praise to people within the company who are doing great work.

The Experts Weigh In

Neal Schaffer, CEO, Maximize Your Social

Social Communications 101: Social Media Was Made for People, Not for Businesses

One of the guiding principles that has kept my online communications sane in social media is based on a holistic perspective and understanding the history of social media. As brands and businesses, we are always engaging on consumer's turf when we communicate on any given social network. Remembering this principle will help guide your organization's communication in becoming more selective and effective at what you communicate and how you communicate it.

Unlike the impersonal, anything-is-possible Internet, social media grew to become a predominant form of communication based on the existence of two things: A personal profile and user-generated content attached to that person's profile. Social media began as, and to many people still is, a personal medium for communication. Your business page on Facebook used to be called a Fan Page because fans of famous celebrities organically created Pages to post the latest information about them. The hashtag, which began on Twitter, was used to allow news about a certain subject, such as the San Diego fire which first spawned its use, be found throughout the platform. Instagram, as depicted in its Polaroid-like icon, was only for publishing photos that were actually taken on the same smartphone they were published from. Remembering these "roots" of social media will help align your communications to that of the average social media user, not of a business simply trying to use social media as another corporate communications channel.

Not only was social media made for people, but the data has proven that (surprise!) people have a greater affinity for people than they do for brands. The Edelman Trust Barometer report is an annual reminder of this fact, but just looking at your Facebook News Feed and trusting that the algorithm Facebook uses, which we refer to as Edgerank, shows that only content from brands that pay for the privilege appear in our News Feeds. We have a deeper relationship with, and engage more with content from, other people—our friends, family, co-workers—than we do with content coming from businesses. Facebook rewards successful content creators by showing their content to more of their friends in their news feeds. With more and more businesses publishing more and more content vying for the attention of the social media user, it's no surprise that the reach of social media content for businesses will continue to decrease and that increasing budgets in Paid Social will be the only way to guarantee that your content gets seen at all.

This doesn't mean that companies can't be effective in social media, as many are, but those that are tend to do one thing well: Humanize their presence. Whether it's showing "behind the scenes" images, live streaming an event from a smartphone, including emoji in their postings, or even posting an image displaying a motivational quote, companies that communicate well in social media not only are removing the distance their brand once had from the social media user, but are also emulating how other social media users act on social media. In other words, they are taking a human approach to social media communication, an approach that almost looks like a foreign language when compared to the traditional web copy branding guidelines most companies created before the advent of social media. Companies need to have this type of unique "voice" in social media, and an even greater challenge is that they similarly need a unique "visual voice" for visual social networks.

Humanizing the content and tone of one's communication in social media will help you become a much better communicator. However, companies do get into the "rut" of creating editorial calendars days, weeks, and sometimes even a few months in advance. The problem is not only that social media is real time, but also that your content is always competing with content from everyone around you.

Take a look at your editorial calendar and ask yourself these three questions:

1. Is your content humanized?
2. Is the tone of your conversation similar to how other people communicate in social media?
3. Can your content compete with organic content from friends of your fans?

Only publish content in social media that can receive a "Yes" answer to all three of these questions. Businesses can never be too human in their tone and content when engaging with social media users.

Priya Ramesh, Director, External Communications, IBM

Taking Your Stories to the Next Level in the Cognitive Era

Let me start by asking you a question. When was the last time you felt so connected with a branded content that it pulled your heart strings and not just compelled you to share that piece of content with your friends and followers online but also turned you into an ambassador or an advocate for that brand or cause? I am pretty sure it did happen and the reason it happened is because that brand or cause had a master storytelling team behind it. Welcome to the era of brand journalism, where press releases are morphing into powerful customer success stories and traditional PR departments are transforming into content studios. Companies like IBM, Coca Cola, Redbull, and Northface are the pioneers of brand storytelling and paved the way for traditional PR and marketing to transform into digital content factories, re-purposing critical marketing budgets to build in-house video and graphic design teams to support the storytelling process.

Let's first understand how the audience mindset has evolved in the last decade, forcing us to rethink how we engage with them. Social media and mobile media have completely revolutionized how companies educate, engage, and empower their key stakeholders. Today, we need to get our message across in 140 characters, in most cases through a powerful visual or a video to an always-on audience that has an attention span of less than ten seconds. Doesn't that feel like hiking Mt. Everest without an oxygen tank? Beyond the digital tsunami created by social and mobile, as modern communicators we are now entering the Cognitive Era, a term coined by IBM Chairwoman and CEO, Ginni Rometty. The Cognitive Era is marked by the convergence of man and machine where every business decision will be aided by a cognitive system. Our customers are now directly talking to Watson, Alexa, and Siri to find information rather than manually searching on a mobile or a desktop device. So the million-dollar question that we must ask ourselves moving beyond the digital to the cognitive age is, "What content do I want to create and how do I deliver it to my audience that now has access to cognitive systems to learn and engage with a brand, product, or cause?" More importantly, the cognitive era will also push more and more companies to think and act like media publishers and train their communications teams to be storytellers first.

At IBM, the global communications team takes a very integrated approach to external communications and at the core of every campaign is *content*. We have a global team of marketing and communications professionals that work collaboratively to generate stories that strengthen the IBM brand and also its strategic imperatives: Cloud, Cognitive, and Innovation. We are an extremely data-driven company and, powered by Watson's cognitive capabilities, we have an in-house team of data scientists and analysts that guide our content creation process. Having this data intelligence increases your chance of reaching your audience in the right format, over the right channel, and even at the right time. If you aspire to be a content-driven communications team, you are guaranteed to have more success with a data-driven mindset to content creation and audience engagement. As a technology leader with a global footprint, we have another key component to our storytelling and content creation process; we think digital, mobile, and, more importantly, *local* content. We work very closely with our colleagues worldwide to ensure the stories that we create in the U.S. are also customized to local audiences. Localization is a very critical step in the content marketing process that I am afraid many companies especially those with global audiences seem to miss. The content you generated for a Twitter campaign that was a huge success in the U.S. may fail in China where people do not have access to the platform. So, creating the right content for your target audience in the channel that they mostly engage with is key to your success.

So you have nailed your content strategy, which is backed by sound data intelligence, and you have developed amazing content that you think your target audience is going to absolutely love. Now what? Content creation is just the first phase. The real magic happens when you have given your story the wings it needs to fly high. Socializing your content internally with your employees is *the* most important first step. In some cases, this might even be a litmus test for your content. Your employees also tend to be your harshest critics so if you manage to wow them, chances are you will have that much more success with your external audiences. Adweek recently published a case study on how IBM successfully got 1,000 staffers to become brand advocates on social media. In 2014, we launched a business-to-business appeal called #NewWayToWork, which garnered over 120 million digital impressions and drove 141,000 clicks to campaign content, largely by IBM employees. This is just one example of the many ways in which IBM has made empowering its own people base with social content a priority. Your employees are your biggest brand advocates and when you engage and empower them with great content, you give your story that much more ignition power to reach new heights.

Last but never the least, be it the digital or cognitive age, keep in mind you are still trying to reach and engage with a human being at the end of it all, not a machine. So let's try to tell stories that touch that human heart or inspire that human mind and give them a very good reason to love your brand.

Ai Ching Goh, CEO and Co-Founder, Piktochart

Cultivate Company Culture with Storytelling

Storytelling might be the most important skill in the twenty-first-century startup's marketing kit. In the context of a startup, telling stories the right way helps with public relations, and it aids in helping a brand establish its own unique personality.

Although user stories are one of the most popular forms of storytelling in a startup, it's also important to look at stories you tell internally. As every startup grows, there's the risk of each "organ" functioning independently, and every organization can only scale when they are united.

When our Piktochart team was smaller in size, I found it easier to tell stories internally—I conveyed my worries, my hopes, and my desires to see the company take a certain form or follow a particular vision. Storytelling was easy when you could still gather around an invisible "campfire" and share war stories.

For example, our reason for not taking funding for four years has been an unconventional one, and from time to time, we still find our team asking us, "Why aren't we hiring twice as many people?" These stories needed to be told again and again.

There are a few things that I felt were important in storytelling to my team:

- Be authentic to the point of vulnerability.
- Repeat important aspects and over-communicate.
- Accept that not everyone is going to like the story you are going to tell and move on.

I strive to be honest and transparent with my internal team to the point of vulnerability. There were two quarters when we did not do as well as I had expected financially, and I got straight to the point. Although the message wasn't necessarily disciplinary in tone, I also still had to make sure that the team understood the situation and would try to work together to find ways of overcoming the challenge. It was also better for my vision to be out there and survive all comments than for it to remain in my head where it was safe and no one could offer his or her feedback.

In most of my messages, I create a Piktochart presentation of what needs to be presented. Then, I send it over to a team of leaders for feedback and proofreading before presenting it during a "town hall" meeting. I found that it has been important to repeat the message at least two times for important announcements, as people seem to always still have questions even during a third presentation.

I do not consider myself a great storyteller, but I have found that the team will always listen with great intent to the story that is being told. They appreciate any information that I give them. There have been many times when I tried thinking about how to deliver a message so that it would not offend people, and I've tried mightily to please the listeners. There is a very fine balance between being assertive and a great listener.

What the leaders do also trickles down throughout an organization. As we are doing our best to share and "open up" within the organization, there are various things that our team members have also adopted. Our communication channels range from:

- Whole organization
    - *Monday town halls:* All the major announcements happen here, from new hires and project updates to financial performance and recaps of marketing recaps. They're the best way to monitor the pulse of how Piktochart is doing.

    - *Wednesday lunch and learns:* This started out as a way for people to have some stage time to share about their topics of interest. We've since incorporated Ask Piktochart Anything and Ask Me Anything into our Wednesday Lunch and Learn sessions.
    - *Nerds, our internal blog:* An internal platform where team members can share all kinds of lessons that they have learned from the launch of campaigns, switching technology stacks, or perhaps even the rationale behind starting a particular campaign. This helps to celebrate efforts that may not be seen on a daily basis but can also document some very important lessons from which everyone can learn. Selected technical articles can also be featured on our medium publication and our main blog!
    - *Weekly email recaps:* This email comes from me and has a recap of important metrics like weekly sign ups, revenue, costs, and project updates (again) as well as new templates, blog articles, press mentions, and the top infographics created by our users.
- Individual level
    - *Peer-to-peer review:* Twice a year, our team members can select who they would like to leave an encouraging comment for (as well as give feedback for their improvement).
    - Recognizing people's efforts publicly via Kudos—an internal platform where everyone gets a monthly allotment of points that they can give out to their peers for a job well done. These points can be redeemed in the form of rewards like a "Pikto-boy band concert" or a donation to various charities.
- Individual to company
    - *Anonymous bi-weekly Slackbot surveys:* This is how we find out how we're doing as a company. The culture/temperature in a company shifts over time.

Communication is the lifeline that helps a startup to function. Without it, all the different "organs" of a startup will function independently, and it will cause the whole organization to act incoherently and ultimately fail.

Here's a quote from one of our team mates, Marta, on the importance of storytelling:

I thought of one great example of storytelling in Piktochart. It was when Laura, our User researcher, introduced Humans of Piktochart. It became my favorite presentation because those were real stories of real people using Piktochart. The purpose was to get everyone on the same page, get to know "personas" really well so that each of us could adapt this knowledge to their work. Storytelling made it unique and engaging! It helped to obtain buy-in from various teams.

Notes

1 Sheree Johnson, SJ Insights, "New Research Sheds Light on Daily Ad Exposures," September 29, 2014. Available at: https://sjinsights.net/2014/09/29/new-research-sheds-light-on-daily-ad-exposures/ (accessed May 22, 2017).

2 Kevin McSpadden, *Time Health*, "Now You Have a Shorter Attention Span Than a Goldfish," May 14, 2015.

3 Native Advertising Roundup, eMarketer, October 2014, p. 2. Available at: www.emarketer.com/public_media/docs/eMarketer_Native_Advertising_Roundup.pdf (accessed May 22, 2017).

4 Kashmir Hill, "#McDStories: When a Hashtag Becomes a Bashtag," *Forbes*, January 24, 2012.

5 Brian Solis and Deirdre Breakenridge, *Putting the Public Back in Public Relations* (New York: FT Press, April 2009), 101.

Chapter 5

Owning Your Brand and Your Reputation

At the end of the day, you're responsible for how you represent your brand and the digital footprint you create. When you post information in different communities you're leaving a trail of breadcrumbs for people to find you through the search engines. Social media has become an easy and popular way for people to access news and information. According to the American Press Institute, Millennials get approximately 88 percent of their news from Facebook.[1] At the same time, people will openly talk about you and share their thoughts related to your brand and your work, regardless of whether it has your stamp of approval. Technically you lose "control" of your brand and any communication about you the minute the sharing begins. All the more reason to focus on the importance of monitoring and protecting your reputation at all times.

Having a public brand means opening up the flood gates, from the very positive critique to the negative information you sometimes don't want to hear. The bottom line is that all the feedback, including harsh criticism, is a gift. With this amazing gift you have a choice. You can use it to help build a stronger brand and closer relationships, or you can ignore what is being said, and take a risk on the backlash that may ensue.

Increasing your digital footprint can also be a positive experience. Whether it is your company or your own professional brand, there are so many opportunities to create, connect, and share via different media channels, building your brand advocates. Your brand can go much further than you would ever expect when you enlist the support of your champions who know and trust you. Suddenly your targeted local effort grows to global scale overnight. For this very reason, you have to be a smart sharer and build a "Reputation Task Force" to keep a watchful eye and help champion your brand online.[2]

The questions and answers in this chapter will help you to understand the best ways to build and elevate your brand, monitor your interactions, and stay close to your audience's reactions. Even though you "own" your brand and your reputation, don't ever forget it is your customers and all the people you interact with who really share a role in shaping your image and helping you to grow. At the end of the day, your experiences with others, through their eyes, will determine how much or how little people want to be a part of who you are and what you do online and offline too. When you own your brand and share the right way, you and your reputation will thrive.

Question 109. Why Should You be the Lead of the Brand Called "Me?"

Personal or professional branding is your job. You have to treat your own brand as a business, realizing you are the Chief Reputation Officer (CRO) ready to maintain, protect, and create opportunities for advancement. Your brand is what you stand for and how others will see you in your career. Everything you do leaves a long trail to you and your digital properties.

Here's who will be watching and hopefully reaching out as a result of you tending to your brand:

- companies interested in working with you;
- professionals and industry contacts who want to build a relationship and align their own brands to you;
- prospective employees, if you own your own business;
- potential partners looking to collaborate on interesting projects;
- HR professionals and executive search firms seeking talent for various positions;
- soon-to-be advocates and champions who want to learn more about you and share your thought leadership;
- journalists, bloggers, and other influencers who may want to contact you for interviews, stories, and events.

Any or all of these people will be watching where you have been, and what you have done. But, most of all, your brand will help them to see where you are going.

Your brand showcases your strengths, growth, and personality, from your offline networking to your online and social media presence. Of course, when and how you engage with others will be

Figure 5.1 Taking Care of Your Brand Online

evaluated and, yes, you will be judged. Taking the lead of a brand called "Me" also means monitoring closely what is being said and honestly evaluating how your brand looks and is perceived by others online. This exercise requires that you check your ego at the door. Not taking the lead will eventually decrease your chances for potential opportunity and the relationships that can develop.

By taking on the role as the CRO of your own brand, you will see new doors open, leading you down the path of greater professional growth and new career opportunities.

Question 110. Why Is It Important to Always Build Bridges and Not Burn Them?

The expression "don't burn any bridges," really holds true for your brand throughout your career. You may have heard the familiar saying, "it's a small world" and you're always six degrees of separation away from anyone. Building bridges is a great way to extend your relationships and even mend those that are strained.[3]

With high journalist turnover rates and publications downsizing, you never know where your media contacts will land for their next opportunity. Brand journalism is also on the rise and many journalists are crossing the chasm over to the field of PR, landing in-house marketing/PR content positions. Changing technology, consumer behavior, and the media landscape drive this change. At some point, these once-known media colleagues may even become your communication peers.[4] Remember, if you choose to burn a bridge, then you just never know where or when your contacts will resurface in your career and what kind of reaction they will have when they interact with you.

The social media world is even smaller. Here is a perfect example. I have a friend, Bill*, who shared a story about a bitter employee that left his company. The employee decided to speak negatively about Bill amongst a group of online friends. The angry individual thought he was sharing information with an "intimate" circle of close friends. However, Facebook is never as private as you might think. Anyone can screenshot what you share.

Not knowing Bill had been privy to the negative discussion about him, that same employee decided to list him as a reference on his resume. Well, you can imagine what Bill did when he received the call from a potential employer asking about this former employee's work history. It was a really short call. The details of employment were given, but certainly no glowing praise.

In every case, always work hard to build bridges and never burn them. Who you are and how you handle relationships will follow you around throughout your career. Your relationships are a direct reflection on you.

Question 111. What Does It Take to Maintain and Protect a Company's Reputation?

If you work at a company, then your PR or communications team cannot be the only brand champions, protecting and maintaining the organization's reputation. It takes an army on the inside to support and believe in the brand. These employee champions become your vocal advocates. At the same time, you can also have public champions who are more than happy to lend a hand. They, too, will jump into conversations and situations to defend your brand and good honor.

In some cases, these champions are your own customers who have consistent, positive experiences with you. They are ready to "protect and serve" at all costs. These are the customers who are deemed your true "Passionates." They go to great lengths to build you up in their communities and protect your integrity at all times.

You can also build strong relationships with your influential media friends. When trouble strikes, it's important to have media "friends" who will be willing to hear and report your side of the

*I've changed the name of my friend to "protect the innocent." Yes, it's an even smaller PR world.

story, especially when issues arise. Many social media influencers, including bloggers and other trusted, influential individuals with large social network communities, are also a conduit to sharing accurate information. Creating relationships with these influencers helps to disseminate messages quickly and amplify to larger groups.

Involving your "village" means you must expand past the marketing and PR professionals to make sure you have champions on the inside and externally too. Here's a checklist of champions to see if you are truly connected and utilizing your village:

- people in your communities who you respect and trust, regardless of the size of their network;
- well-known personalities, but not quite celebrities, who are popular and drive important conversations;
- customers who are your advocates and brand champions ready to defend you;
- employees at your company in different departments (beyond marketing) proud of the brand they have helped to build;
- journalists and members of the media who follow your news and report on your stories.
- bloggers, YouTubers, Instagrammers, etc., who are well known and respected community members;
- analysts who feed the financial community and who you regularly keep informed about your company growth and new product development;
- partners, vendors, and service providers who have had a great experience working with you.

They say it takes a village to raise a child; well it is no different for a brand.

Question 112. How Do You Avoid the Blacklist?

You don't want to end up on one of *those* lists. There have been countless instances where communicators are "blacklisted," whether it was by editors at mainstream publications or bloggers who felt the PR people they knew kept making the same pitching mistakes over and over again.[5] Because you live in a small media world, news about your organization or your own professional conduct can spread quickly and not always in the most flattering light.

The best way to stay off the blacklist is to build good relationships from the beginning. From the intelligence you uncover and the first pitch to your initial conversations, these interactions set the tone for the rest of your exchanges. Your reputation will remain credible and trustworthy if you provide accurate information and follow through as a helpful and consistent resource. Anything less than credible and trustworthy may result in the blacklist.

Since I have been blogging, and more recently podcasting, the tables for me as a PR person have turned. I'm receiving pitches daily. Just through my experience as a "media" person fielding pitches, here are a few of the tactics to avoid the blacklist:

1. Don't reach out with a form letter, especially if you forget the mail merge and the email says, "Dear [first name] [last name]."
2. Don't pull together one big list of media/blogger emails and mass "spam" everyone on the list. Not only is it annoying, but people receiving the pitch prefer that you do not share their email address openly for all to see. This is a general rule for any emails. If this is the case, then it is time to invest in email marketing software such as Constant Contact, iContact, or MailChimp, so you can personalize emails to all of your contacts.
3. Don't send a pitch that has nothing to do with the media person's community. I've actually received pitches for pet and beauty products to be shared on my blog, PR Expanded. Although I love animals and appreciate skincare and makeup, I still can't figure out the angles.
4. Don't make the journalist figure out the angle. Your job is to be clear and compelling. The unique story angle should be "jumping off the page."
5. Don't harass anyone if they decide not to cover your story. If someone nicely declines, be happy they were pleasant about saying, "no." Emailing, trying to call, or pinging them publicly on social media won't work either.

Start the relationship the right way, be reliable, and let the relationship progress from there. Aside from staying off the blacklist, you'll see a "thank you" come in the form of a healthy and long-term relationship.

Question 113. Can PR Fix a Broken Brand?

Today, your brand is in your customers' hands. You no longer own it, they do. Because your reputation belongs to them, too, you must deliver on every claim and celebrate your customers with great information and impeccable service. You can have the best PR in the world. However, great PR will not erase a bad experience due to a poorly made, low-quality product. Add into the mix ongoing lousy customer service and a bad situation just became ten times worse.

Using PR as a "cover-up" approach will backfire in the end. PR builds awareness, credibility, and big expectations. But, a company or a brand that cannot deliver what it promises through PR, no matter how strong the promotional activities and media coverage, in the end will face a damaged reputation. The market and company stakeholders are forgiving only to a point. Do not expect your PR program to build a good reputation and positive public opinion, when your company is not delivering on its promise or creating good experiences across the board. PR alone can't fix a broken brand.

Years ago, I took on a project with a tech brand that couldn't figure out why they had great PR and marketing, but nothing was translating into new leads and sales. We took an investigative approach and decided to evaluate what a new prospect experienced once they learned about the company through the PR coverage. We employed some "mystery shoppers." These shoppers contacted the company via links offered on the landing pages from different promotions, as well as links they found in their Google searches. It ended up that nine out of ten mystery shoppers were not able to get through to the company's sales team. Several of them clicked on links that were broken or no longer active. Others reached out with the telephone numbers offered and found themselves on hold for far too long. One mystery shopper used an "email us" on the contact page of the website, requested a demo, and never heard back from a company representative.

Your PR and marketing may be stellar, but what happens after you get all the coverage and drive people to your website matters too. Be sure to do your part to point out any breaks in the process, so everything and everyone gets connected the right way to fix the broken brand.

Question 114. How Do You Change a "Spin Doctor" Reputation?

Before the start of every show, Bill O'Reilly, former *Fox News* host said, "Caution, you are about to enter the no spin zone." Regardless of how you feel about Bill O'Reilly and *Fox News*, wouldn't it be great

Figure 5.2 The Spin Doctor Reputation

if this were true? News should be objective, delivering the facts and important accurate information to consumers. At the same time, PR should be just as objective, reliable, and trustworthy.

Working in PR, this is a familiar phrase, especially when it comes to your work with the media. Your job is delivering credible and newsworthy information. Credibility may take time to earn, but it can be lost in an instance. In the past, PR people have been seen as "flacks" and masters of "spin." Marketing expert, Gini Dietrich, CEO of Arment Dietrich, wrote her book, *Spin Sucks*, for this very reason. The moniker of "spin" is not the reputation modern communicators have worked so hard to build.

However, saying you are not a Spin Doctor just isn't enough. You have to show that "you" are not one. Here are some of the best ways to act or *prove* you are a valuable communicator and news resource:

- share compelling and authentic stories in your communities;
- deliver valuable information consistently and with frequency;
- be timely to help journalists to meet their deadlines;
- work on being a partner with the media by feeding them with information, even when you are not a part of the story;
- refrain from enhancing, inflating, or stretching the truth;
- research and verify sources, making sure they are accurate before you share them with the media;
- have the facts ready and don't promise things you cannot deliver;

- respect the media and the public;
- avoid a mindset that opts for PR stunts and negative publicity just to get news.

When the spin stops, you'll see the media and the public pay attention. With all the spin that is out there now it may be hard to believe this, but people remember the authentic and credible information you share. As a communicator, you need to be a sentinel of the "no spin zone."

Question 115. Can a Bad Experience Leave a Black Mark on a Brand?

After business executives have a "bad" experience with PR and marketing professionals, it's difficult to convince them there's value working with outside communication counsel. For example, when it is a company's second or even third time around with a new agency (after being burned once or twice), there may be reservations. With companies that are hesitant, it is best to start out slowly, listen carefully, and set the appropriate expectations. Big retainer fees become taboo and suddenly the words "project fees" are much more tolerable. But, remember, the proof that PR and marketing are valuable can only be found in the depth of the relationships, the credibility you bring to the table, and the trust that forms, all to deliver the tangible results.

In my experience, whether it is a new agency client or you are working with your own in-house team, you can make colleagues feel comfortable about PR and marketing by recommending a shorter time frame for a program and/or testing a market with a campaign, before making a full commitment and a larger investment. With the option to review and continue, when expectations are met (and hopefully exceeded), the hesitations will subside and the PR and marketing programs will prove their worth.

However, there are times when the black mark sticks and minds won't be changed. I was approached to develop a two-year marketing program for an agency. As a consultant, I pulled together a team of qualified professionals, including a boutique agency, who would execute the PR and social media part of the program. After gathering the key players, creating the proposal, and discussing a rough budget estimate, my in-house contact came back to me with an "issue." He explained how the CEO, who had the final say, was opposed to working with consultants due to some very bad past experiences.

The fact here was that I was a consultant and I couldn't change this. No matter my credentials or the "A" team I pulled together for the company. Just the word "consultant" came with a big black mark. A perfect case of a few consultants leaving the black mark, shutting down the possibility of working with future consultants who might bring tremendous value to the organization.

When it comes to reputation and the black mark, it is very real and it can be a long and ever-lasting mark on your brand.

Question 116. Does "No comment" Mean You Are Hiding Something?

As a communicator, you may need to manage questions which are difficult for your company or your client to answer. Media training prepares company spokespeople to respond properly to tough questions. Training teaches professionals to redirect the conversation away from the "sticky" and often reputation-damaging information to the accurate and timely details that can be released publicly.

Because "No comment" may imply you are hiding something, executives or company representatives must learn how to answer questions without saying, "No comment." There are other ways to explain that you are unable to provide the media with information. When you want to say, "No comment," use another acceptable and/or transparent phrase, such as:

1. "I don't have that information right now, but will share it with you as soon as it is available."
2. "We'll be answering those types of questions shortly" (but then get ready to release the information or answers relatively soon).
3. "This is not the case, but what I can tell you is …"
4. "I'm happy to get that information to you."
5. "That's not my area of expertise, but what I do know is …"

Whether your "No comment" means you have the information and you cannot share it due to timing constraints, or you just don't know at that very instant, it is best to rephrase your response in a more transparent and accurate way. Your goal is to stay transparent, helpful, and ready to provide more information, when you can and as often as necessary.

Question 117. What Do You Think about Always Being "Nice?"

An old friend and a former employee of mine shared a blog post story about how you should always be nice. She said being nice or pleasant in your interactions is such a simple lesson. This is true, you know you can attract more bees with honey. In her post, she reminisced about a memory working at my old agency in New Jersey. One of our co-workers had been working a client's story with the media and found herself having a really tough time with one particular journalist.

Although she was as pleasant as anyone could be under the circumstances, there was a less than pleasant media professional on the other end of the telephone line. After hanging up the phone with the journalist, she turned to us and said, "Why can't people be nice all of the time?" She certainly was pleasant all the time, even when she was having the worst day. The difference … she never took it out on anyone else.

Fast forward 15 years later to a media event I attended in New York City. A panel of *Fortune* editors shared stories about PR professionals and entrepreneurs who pitched them. The editors appeared to be very friendly and sounded helpful when it came to the good pitches they received. However, if they were not interested in a pitch, then they would simply not respond to the person pitching the story angle. Sounds logical.

One editor shared a story about a young entrepreneur who over-pitched him and his colleagues, simultaneously. When the entrepreneur did not receive an answer to his pitch, he started to send very nasty emails to the editor. He questioned why he was not receiving a response from anyone at *Fortune*. Here is a case of: you may think your story is super important but not everyone else does. Bothering people to the point of harassment will definitely not increase their interest or get you a feature story.

How far do you think this entrepreneur's story went? Do you think it ever appeared in the publication? Absolutely not. The pitch made it into the email trash bin. The lesson to be remembered … being nice goes both ways, no matter who is on deadline or stressed out due to their work circumstances. In this example, the entrepreneur's reputation was tarnished in the eyes of several editors at *Fortune*. All it took was one email correspondence that went down the less-than-nice path.

The rule is, no matter what, just be nice … your reputation depends on it.

Question 118. Can You Change or Rebuild Your Reputation?

You can be on top of the world, with a great career, family, and life. One mistake leads to another on an ethical slippery slope, and suddenly there's a compound effect. Years ago, I watched a Pharmaceutical CEO move from media darling to "bad" guy in the news, after an extra-marital affair with a co-worker became public information. Scandal. Unfortunately, he lost his job, his family, and the stress of the situation may have resulted in serious illness. He passed away from cancer several years later. This was a very sad and unfortunate story, with an unhappy ending.

However, I have also seen an executive go from having to serve time in prison to becoming a rehabilitated, caring, and hard-working professional, ready to give back and rebuild his reputation. So, yes, you can change or rebuild your reputation when your heart and mind are in the right place. It also requires a great deal of hard work to not be branded as a "former felon peddling his story of woe." In 2014, an ex-international arms sales executive contacted me. He had pleaded guilty to conspiracy to pay foreign bribes, illegally exporting controlled goods without authorization, and falsifying books and records. He had read my books in prison and needed help answering media interviews and rebuilding his messaging and reputation after his release.

After reading the court documents, I believed 100 percent in this executive's full rehabilitation, as well as his sincere desire to make a positive contribution to society by using his experience as a real-world example for those who face similar challenges in their work. I decided to work with him to formulate the messaging around the circumstances of his imprisonment and his new mission to educate others moving forward. We took many steps to get his reputation back intact and to align his story with themes and examples from his experience as positive pivot points.

During the transformation, he worked tirelessly to create original blog content and to share valuable information, all for teaching and mentoring others about a journey that was now in his "rear view mirror." Incredibly, he had no fee schedule. His initial commitment was to talk about his perspective for the first year to anyone who thought it might be helpful. He first wanted to see if he could add value to what was already a very engaged anti-bribery compliance field. The decision to build a practice would come years later.

As an FCPA (Foreign Corrupt Practices Act) and anti-bribery compliance blogger, his blog posts began to push down the negative articles due to timeliness and relevancy. As he spoke at different events and global symposiums, new photos replaced the less flattering ones. It was also his pleasant and helpful attitude that got him recognized by major media outlets, conference organizations, and even international enforcement agencies that wanted to work with him. He went from not having a Twitter account in 2012/2013 during his incarceration, to being verified by Twitter in 2016. He was also recognized in 2015 by a global ethics organization as one of the top 100 business people in ethical influence.

Not once did this executive tire of sharing the details of his story. With transparency, he gave the specifics and framed out why this much-needed information would help other professionals and organizations to be more compliant, and to understand behavioral risk far away from home. For him, the work to rebuild his reputation was abundant and time-consuming, but the results surpassed all our expectations. He became a recognized expert source. Today, prestigious media outlets, large organizations, and ethical governing bodies are turning to this client for information and advice on anti-bribery and FCPA compliance issues.

With the return of his passport in 2017, after the expiry of his federal probation, it is almost a new beginning, as he takes his practice and experience to where it is needed most: the front-lines of international business.

Question 119. How Important Is Brand Consistency for Your Reputation?

Very important. If you have a number of channels that all have different logos, imagery, and inconsistent brand elements, or your tone, personality, and messaging are inconsistent, then you will end up confusing your audience. The result may be less-than-desired participation or little interest in what you're doing. There is only one you, which needs to be consistent across the board. Consistency is the great re-enforcer of your brand and your reputation.

Here are some questions to ask yourself to make sure your brand is consistent throughout your online and social media properties.

- Are you using approved brand imagery and do you have access to a repository of approved content?
- Are you using the official company logo or an approved version of the logo?

Figure 5.3 Keeping Your Brand Consistent

- Is the color scheme on your social media properties identical or near identical to your corporate/brand colors?
- Are you sharing information that supports your brand and thought leadership with topics that help your customers at every communication touch point?
- Do you have community managers who know the characteristics, tone, and language of your brand?
- Do the people who officially represent your brand uphold your brand values and protect your reputation across all channels?
- When people interact with you online and through social media, do they have the same experience when they meet you or a company representative in person?

The people who know you and have interacted in different places (online and offline) expect something from you, at every touch point. This is a part of your brand promise. Confusing people through your channels, including social media, is not living up to your promise and may hurt your image and reputation. As a result, you may lose potential customers and disappoint loyal advocates. Who you are online is who you are offline, at all times, with no exceptions.

Question 120. How Do You Keep "Good Company" Online and Through Social Media?

One way to keep good company is to "question" the people who connect to you. For example, guest blog post scams are more numerous today. The individuals behind the scams are taking greater lengths to get published. I remember one incident that had me going back and forth with someone, let's call her "LC," who was trying to get some guest posts on my blog. For the sake of educating others about the experience, I went along with the scam up to the point when LC asked, "I offered you decent articles for free and you act suspicious? Why is that?"

There are plenty of reasons to act suspicious to protect my reputation, which I'll explain shortly. But, first, here were the red flags that helped me to keep my brand in good company:

Red flag 1 When LC reached out as an experienced writer and the editor of a business publication, she wanted to contribute several articles to my blog, PR Expanded. I immediately Googled her and she didn't exist. I checked LinkedIn and there was no LC with her image and the credentials she shared.

Red flag 2 was the photo that accompanied LC's email. The image of the person in the photo looked more like a 16-year-old high school student. She was wearing a teeny weeny little tank top as if she was going to the beach with her friends. LC's image was completely incongruous with the article topics and her claimed experience in business. I told LC that the picture was not quite right for the article and I needed to see a few business head shots.

Red flag 3 was that LC completely ignored my request.

Red flag 4 was that I noticed an area in the article that didn't make any sense. I asked LC to explain and, she said: "You may add a few sentences to make it work, that's not a problem."

Red flag 5 was that most experienced writers would want to make the edits themselves. It was extremely suspect that someone identified as a business writer and an experienced editor would ***not*** rewrite a section of her own article.

Red flag 6 occurred when I did a little more homework on the link that was used in the article byline. There was only one and when I googled it, the word "*scam*" was tied to every comment and article that I accessed.

Now, to answer LC's question: "I offered you decent articles for free and you act suspicious? Why is that?"

Here is why it is so important for you to be suspicious when it comes to your brand:

- Your friends, partners, clients, organizations, professional affiliations, etc., are a reflection of *you*, whether you like it or not.
- If a brand is linked to you, then the perception may be that you and this brand are connected, perhaps in ways that don't help your brand or reputation.
- You always have to think proactively and clearly about what you say and do, and how you align your brand with others; it is one of the best ways to manage your brand and reputation.

Having my blog and my personal brand linked to an organization that appears to be practicing unethically is not who I am or what I stand for personally or professionally. This article, and the digging I did, serves a dual purpose. The first is to share the warning signs when someone out of the blue offers you a guest post on your blog or website. The second is to remind you that your brand reputation is yours to proactively protect.

Question 121. Will Not Following or Friending Someone on Social Media Look Bad for My Brand or Hurt My Reputation?

You are not obligated to follow back or friend anyone on social media. It is your choice. If you are active on social media, then you need to "screen" your "friends" and your new acquaintances.

Not following or friending is only one step. At the same time, you should also beware of interactions that may also put your brand in a less-than-favorable light.

- *Don't just retweet or reshare someone blindly:* Make sure you check out who you are retweeting or resharing. You can even take it a step further by looking into the source of their information. What you share is ultimately a reflection of you.
- *Don't just use any old hashtag just because someone else did:* You have to investigate what the hashtag stands for and the type of comments and content that is being shared by other people using that same hashtag.

- *Don't hastily answer requests and comments in your newsfeed or your Twitter stream, unless you know who you're answering:* Find out who is posting the question. Of course, you're going to respond to your customers and members in your community in a timely manner. But, there may be times when trolls or detractors will reach out to engage you in "no win" discussions. They try to bait you into less than flattering conversations. You should always monitor what a detractor says, but no direct response is necessary.
- *Don't engage with bots or share fake news:* The easiest way to identify a bot is by checking out its Twitter feed. Bots will often retweet much more than an authentic human account. Another tell-tale sign is they have younger accounts with few followers. Once you identify the bot, you'll also be able to spot the fake news quickly.
- *Don't just follow anyone who follows you:* It is OK if you decide not to follow someone, especially if they don't share information that interests you—or your followers—or support your brand. You can also tell a lot from someone's avatar, profile, and the general nature of the content they share. You're allowed to be selective when it comes to the company you keep.

These "Don'ts" are simple reminders to keep your brand in great company. Remember, like attracts like.

Question 122. What Does It Mean to be True to Your Brand?

People will know your brand based on what they see and experience with you. For these reasons, always stand up for what you believe in and be your own person. Being unique is a way to make your brand stand out from the crowd.

Earlier in my career, I accepted a position that started to erode away at my personal brand. I was running a small PR department for a cosmetology school affiliated with a popular hair and skincare company. Within my first couple of weeks of working there, I was asked to model for a hair fashion show. What happened was an honor, and then quite a shock. On stage, the stylist cut my very long hair to a short cut, above my ears. He colored my hair from dark brown to bright red. At the time, the transformation did not look like me or feel like me either.

After the show, there were some strict requirements pertaining to the way I looked:

1. *Required hairstyle:* I had to keep my hair short and continued with the red color to "fit in" with the culture.
2. *Required makeup:* Management suggested I use the makeup and colors that were more representative of the company.
3. *Required clothing:* I also learned that they wanted me to wear only black and white clothing, to mirror my colleagues.

All three requirements told me one thing ... This just wasn't me! I eventually realized I was not being true to myself or to my own brand.

Almost like a *Devil Wears Prada* movie scenario with Anne Hathaway and Meryl Streep, although I didn't dramatically throw my mobile phone into a fountain, I left the company and got reacquainted with my own brand. I grew out my hair, went back to my natural hair color, and found my own style of fashion.

If I could go back in time and give advice to my younger self, I would say, "Be true to who you are and your brand, from the work you do to how you present yourself (including your appearance), in any role you play."

Question 123. Why Should You Create a Reputation-monitoring Checklist?

You cannot leave reputation monitoring to chance in an age of online and social conversations. Just because you are not active in certain social media communities does not mean that people are not talking about you. The best approach is to put a five-step process in place to make sure you are catching what is being said about you, and then take the appropriate actions.

Step 1 is to set up simple monitoring with keywords that relate to you or your brand. Your monitoring could be as simple as Google Alerts, or using a social search engine that allows you to set up notices every time your name or your keywords are mentioned.

Step 2 is to frequently Google yourself to see how you appear online and through social media.

Step 3 is to make sure you check under News, Images and Videos on Google or other search engines to see if anyone else has posted unflattering visuals and information on your behalf.

Step 4 is to build strong relationships proactively in your communities. Having many champions around you, who believe in your brand, is a proactive step toward reputation management. These champions will stand up for you when others attack your character or even question your reputation.

Step 5, which is the most important step to keep your reputation intact, is to make sure you are acting ethically. You also have to communicate responsibly, at all times, in your communities and treat people with the dignity and the respect they deserve.

The steps on your monitoring checklist go a long way to proactively protecting your reputation and perhaps even preventing unnecessary reputation damage.

Question 124. When Do You Stop Beta Testing?

Companies and their brands cannot be static; they change and grow every day. Today, loyal fans interact with their brands through different touch points. These advocates are happy to engage and share feedback, all to create better experiences with you.

Your brand should always be in the Beta testing phase. A New Balance (NB) campaign stated on its website how their brand is "Always in Beta." NB realizes there is "no finish line to improvement." You can't stop creating and innovating just because your customers are satisfied and your sales are good. On the contrary, because the marketplace faces many changes, whether these are economic, regulatory, political, or technological, you should be in Beta to make sure your stakeholders are happy and actively championing for you.[6]

Professional brands should be in a constant state of Beta too. When professionals reinvent themselves over time, whether they expand their areas of expertise or want to rebrand their image as they grow in their careers, this is also Beta testing in action. I've been beta testing and transforming my brand for years. Here's how my story progressed:

1. contributing writer to various publications
2. Prentice Hall, Financial Times Press and Routledge print / online book author

3. PR 2.0/PR expanded blogger
4. Lynda.com/LinkedIn Learning video author
5. Women Worldwide podcaster
6. FB live digital correspondent.

Thankfully, throughout my transformation, my clients, colleagues, peers, friends, etc., have given me the gift of critique, at every significant benchmark in my progression.

You need to move, morph, and grow, making sure you involve your community along the way. Beta testing will always lead to better transformation and brand growth.

Question 125. How Does Social Media Help You to Avoid Brand Damage?

Social media helps to maintain a reputation through consistent, frequent, and transparent communication with customers, media, analysts, bloggers, and other important stakeholders.

Social media communication gives a brand a voice, a face, and human emotions. For example, if there is an apology due, then seeing a CEO or spokesperson address a situation and offer a mea culpa is much more believable than a canned, written statement in a news release. Of course, in many cases, regardless of the channel, a PR team may be behind the communication. But it is the emotion and sincerity, which still comes through with body language and facial expressions to deliver a heartfelt apology.

In addition, when you engage in social media communication, your brand becomes a member of a community. If you have a good reputation and you're providing the community with important information (not "spammy" marketing messages), your advocates will come to your aid, should your reputation or image be challenged. These loyal enthusiasts will set the community straight and help to clear up any communication that is not accurate.

From personal experience, I know the power of community. As an active professional on Twitter, a troll or what I reference as a "Deterrent Detractor," decided to share some unpleasant thoughts about me that were not true. It was inflammatory and highly offensive. The rule with trolls is not to engage and to just listen and monitor what they are saying. Thankfully, several community members jumped in to chase the troll away. Going the extra mile, one of my Twitter friends did some research on the troll to expose that "she" had an alias, and was actually an unhappy professional in our industry. I was surprised at the situation. At the same time, I was very thankful for the power of community.

Social media and my community of supporters helped me move through a challenging situation, safeguarding my reputation along the way.

Question 126. How Do You Know If You Are Dealing with a Crisis That Could Damage Your Reputation?

First off, there are clear differences between an issue and a crisis. You can anticipate and identify issues selectively. Issues can also be an opportunity to turn a negative occurrence into a positive learning situation.[7] However, a true crisis can have severe ramifications for both your reputation and your bottom line revenue. I learned early on that there are definitely warning signs and questions that you need to ask yourself to determine if you're dealing with a crisis that is quickly unfolding.

Here are several of the questions you can ask yourself and, based upon your "yes" or "no" response, you should be able to determine quickly if you are dealing with a volatile crisis situation.

- Will the current situation damage the company's reputation, or will there be financial repercussions?
- Is the media knocking on your door for answers to questions, or do you have bloggers reaching out through social media for comments? If you're a company that usually has to approach the media to pitch a story and suddenly everyone is after you for interview, then you may have a crisis on your hands.
- Is this an unfamiliar situation? Is it a situation that you've never experienced before? If you're familiar and you know the steps to resolve the situation, then chances are you're dealing with an issue rather than a crisis.
- Is the situation a surprise, such as an act of nature, a human-made disaster or a situation that is beyond your control?
- Do you feel a loss of control over quickly unfolding events? Is the situation escalating very quickly, and, as a result, it is extremely difficult to combat all the erroneous stories, rumors, and speculation that are already occurring?
- Is there a sense of panic at your company and do you find that your leadership is not wanting to take immediate action?

If you answer yes to any of these questions, then you probably have a crisis that is escalating or one that is already full blown. Be sure to communicate with speed and accuracy and always offer the facts and credible information. Most of all, be sure to tell your own story. You need to stay ahead of the crisis with frequent communication that helps you to move toward quicker resolution.

Question 127. What Is the Best Approach to Crisis?

The best approach to crisis is to get AHEAD. You have a small window of opportunity to tell your own story rather than the media, competitors, customers, or anyone else who may speculate on your behalf. The get AHEAD approach focuses on being forthright, having swift intelligence gathering, sharing critical *need to know information,* and keeping all of your stakeholders well informed in a timely manner.

When crisis strikes, you have to get in front of the story and communicate the facts. It's really important to let the people who need to hear from you know that you're quickly working toward a resolution. If you communicate often and provide critical updates to these audiences throughout the crisis, you're appreciated by the public for your actions and, most of all, your transparency.

At the same time, you want to be closely monitoring conversations online and through your social media channels. You don't want to be thinking about how to measure the effectiveness of your crisis communications while the crisis is unfolding. When crisis strikes, you need to be ready and fully present as a helpful resource, also making sure you are correcting any misinformation related to the situation at hand.

Here are five simple steps to be proactive and to get AHEAD of any crisis situation:

1. *A* is for *Anticipate* what could happen. You're armed with the tools and technology that allow you to hear what people are saying and catch information in the moment the situation occurs or takes a turn for the worse.
2. *H* is to *Head off* and acknowledge what is happening, so your customers and other important constituents know you are on top of the situation and will be providing more details as they become available.
3. *E* is to *Evaluate* and assess the situation carefully. It is imperative to get your facts straight and to understand the many details of the situation before you officially communicate on behalf of your company.

4. *A* is to *Act* quickly and implement your crisis strategy. Speed is of the essence with social media and a very dynamic public who may want to be more involved in an unfolding situation. Citizen journalists are tied to their mobile devices, capturing every moment of crisis with their cameras and through videos. Regardless of their sharing, it is your communication that is imperative and is expected in a timely manner.
5. *D* is to *Determine* success by measuring your efforts. Without measuring the effectiveness of your communication, you will never know if you are neutralizing the situation or if it is escalating even further. You want to make sure you're changing the negative to more positive commentary as you strive to keep your reputation intact.

Every crisis is different and there are different levels of escalations to consider. However, the AHEAD approach is the best way to be in front and to make sure you are telling your own story when a crisis strikes.

The Experts Weigh In

Dorie Clark, Brand Strategist, Author of Stand Out

Associate Yourself with Powerful Brands

Taking a chance on the unknown—whether it's hiring a job applicant, retaining a consultant, or buying an expensive new car—is inherently risky, so customers are looking for signs that they can relax and know that their decision is a wise one.

You can reduce people's concerns about hiring you or doing business with you by leveraging the power of what psychologists call "social proof"—i.e., surrounding yourself with other brands that are already trusted. I learned this early on in my career. Writing a book had been a lifelong goal for me, so one year I made a concerted push: *this would be the year*! I wrote three different book proposals, certain that one would catch a publisher's eye. But they all got rejected, because they said I didn't have a big enough "platform." In other words, I wasn't famous enough for them to take a chance on me.

So, I went back to the drawing board and decided to start blogging. I spent more than a year doing cold pitches and trying to get friends to introduce me to their editors, but finally I was able to break in—first at the *Huffington Post*, then at the *Harvard Business Review*, and later at *Forbes*. The second blog post I ever wrote for the *Harvard Business Review*—about how to reinvent your personal brand—caught on, and they asked me to turn it into a longer piece for their magazine. As soon as it came out, three different literary agents approached me, and I was able to secure a contract for my first book, *Reinventing You*—thanks to the power of "platform" and having a brand name behind me to lend extra credibility.

Stephanie Carls, Customer Success Manager at Rivet, Social Media Correspondent

Owning Your Brand

As I started developing my personal brand, I noticed that it wasn't all about me. It was about delivering value to others. I was still the forefront of the brand, but it wasn't my biggest focus. Demonstrating my value was. I was still letting others know who I was and what I had to offer, but my emphasis was still on others' needs and not my own. I always asked myself if others were experiencing the value I was providing and if they were associating that value with me. One sign of a strong personal brand is always being clear about your unique promise of value—what's authentic to you, differentiating you from your peers, and making you relevant and compelling to your target audience.

Ask yourself some of these questions after every day or week:

1. Did I leave my mark on every meeting I attended—making contributions to the discussion to add value?
2. Did I create and publish content (blog, video, article, whitepaper, etc.), sharing information that will be useful to people who share my expertise?
3. Did I integrate my superpowers—the things I do better than anyone else—into everything I did?
4. Did I share content created by others that is valuable to members of my network? (Bonus points if you add your point of view to the content as well.)

Asking yourself these questions will get you in the habit of contributing. Those contributions—not bragging and shouting—are the foundation for building a strong, enduring personal brand.

Gini Dietrich, CEO of Arment Dietrich, Author of *Spin Sucks*

Be Nice to the Nerds

One of the best business quotes to abide by is, "Be nice to nerds. Chances are you'll end up working for one." Bill Gates said this during a commencement speech many years ago and it rings very true for your brand and your reputation. If you aren't nice to the nerds and you end up working for one someday, imagine how miserable your life will be *and* what kind of reputation you would have among his or her peers.

When I met my husband, I was immediately attracted to the fact that he looked everyone in the eye when he spoke to them. It didn't matter if it was Joe Lieberman (whom he did some work with early in his career) or the busboy at a restaurant. He treated everyone the same. His nickname among his basketball team (I call them the senior NBA) is "Nice Guy Kelly" or NGK for short. It says a lot about his reputation and how he's protected his personal brand.

Imagine if you did the same. It wouldn't matter if you made a mistake—and you will—because people will defend you. Think about that and always be nice to the nerds.

Notes

1 American Press Institute, "How Millennials Use and Control Social Media," March 16, 2015.

2 Deirdre Breakenridge, *Social Media and Public Relations: Eight New Practices for the PR Professional* (New York: FT Press, April 2012), 104.

3 Fiona MacDonald, Science Alert, "Are We Really All Connected by Six Degrees of Separation?", August 2015. Available at: www.sciencealert.com/are-we-all-really-connected-by-just-six-degrees-of-separation (accessed May 17, 2017).

4 Richard Carufel, MediaMiser, "Strained Media Relations: Why Some Journalists Feel Duped by PR Professionals," June 2015.

Available at: www.agilitypr.com/pr-news/social-media/strained-media-relations-why-some-journalists-feel-duped-by-pr-professionals/(accessed May 17, 2017).

5 Chris Anderson, Wired Blog, "Sorry PR People: You're Blocked," October 29, 2007.

6 New Balance Website Homepage, March 2016. Available at: http://www.newbalance.com/ (accessed March 2016).

7 Fraser Seitel, *The Practice of Public Relations* (Upper Saddle River, NJ: Prentice Hall, 2011), 383.

Chapter 6

Measuring Your Success

Why has measurement always been so difficult? A critical part of the modern communicator's role is to be accountable. Measurement must be present in all your programs, tying your communication outreach and engagement to valuable business outcomes. Communicators, especially PR professionals, have the challenge of connecting their communication to higher-level goals and objectives. Your metrics must relate to the financial buckets that hit the bottom line; areas that get the C-Suite's attention.

However, accountability starts with first carving out exactly what is important for either your department and/or what is important for the company on a larger scale. When you know what you're trying to achieve, creating a roadmap or plan lays out the strategy and tactics to help you reach your desired outcomes. From the research, resources, and careful messaging to the channel development and a mix of media, it is a carefully charted course that will lay the groundwork for how you measure and how you show your success.

But, remember, measuring your success for your department and company is also understanding what success looks like to different people in the organization. What executives view as success is different than what the marketing and PR team view as an overall successful program. It is also no surprise that your executives want to receive their information in different ways. The key here is to have a level of accountability across the board, with the appropriate reporting for the right people. Your measurement has to be built into your programs and benchmarked at determined intervals for different professionals.

At the same time, measuring success means you should never neglect your own personal or professional goals. When it comes to your development and success it is just that … personal. You should not compare what you have accomplished to anyone else. You have to know exactly what you want to achieve in order to get there. Do you have a plan to stay on course? Your success and how you measure will also change over time because your definition of success will develop at different stages of your career and life. What was once considered professional success at age 20 may not be your idea of success at age 30 or 40, etc. Regardless, you always have to make the time to set your goals and then follow through in a way that allows you to go down the right path and enjoy the results of your hard work.

The questions and answers in this chapter are all based on setting you up for success at work and as you grow as a modern communicator. They are meant to help you find the important tangibles or meaningful outcomes in your business and professional development. The answers will help you to carve out what success can look like for you in a number of ways, and to avoid the many measurement mistakes you have made in the past.

Question 128. What Is the Best Way to Show Value?

With every PR and marketing budget, you're required to justify those dollars and show the value of your service. You have to think like the CFO of the company, as if every dollar was your own. With that in mind, you can't just measure exposure and engagement. These metrics are not enough for the C-suite. You have to ask, "What did the exposure and engagement lead to for the organization?" By answering the question, you can connect what you are doing in communications to higher-level business goals.

Here are three ways to measure success, with Level III clearly demonstrating the business impact.

- *Level I Outputs:* What you create and share. From your blog posts, news releases and videos to the number of Facebook and Twitter updates you post, outputs are what you communicate and how these communication tactics increase or decrease over time.
- *Level II Outtakes:* What people do with the messages they receive. Outtakes represent the many people who share your content, click on your links to learn more, write blog posts about you, or comment on your blog. Your communication inspires people to act in a way in which you can measure their engagement and/or how well your message was received.

- *Level III Outcomes:* What is financially based that is impacting your business. Outcomes vary, from the traffic you drive to your website to the lead generation and sales as a result of your communication. In addition, outcomes can be in the form of great customer satisfaction, positive sentiment and a brand lift, marketing optimization, or increased employee productivity, resulting from your outreach programs and relationship-building practices.

You can find success on different levels. However, C-level executives recognize and really appreciate the communication that shows business value (the "Outcomes" bucket) and that which provides a Return on Investment (ROI), which is a financial outcome.

Question 129. Do the "Little Things" Make You Feel Successful?

The definition of success is different for everyone. The passion that drives you, and the outcome you wish to achieve, is your success. For some this might be financial gain, but for others it is a feeling of satisfaction, knowing that you've made a difference, helping someone advance, changing your world, and the list goes on. You have to ask yourself what makes you the happiest and what excites you the most. People make money every day, but that doesn't mean they feel successful or that they are truly happy every day.

What puts a smile on my face? Sure, my husband and I need to pay the bills, but my biggest success comes in the form of learning, giving, and educating others. I remember when a college student from Grand Canyon University reached out to me to see if I would be interested in a Skype call with him and his team. He explained how he and his classmates were using one of my books for a class project. I responded quickly, letting him know that I would be happy to chat. His reaction was priceless. He quickly emailed me back thanking me and then made sure that I knew that he was "just a senior in college working on a project." I reinforced that I was aware and the exact reason why I said, "Yes," in the first place. For me, working with students is what I really enjoy.

Knowing that this young man and his team were so excited to speak with me and eager to learn, even if it was just for 20 minutes, makes my years of PR more meaningful. It is the "little things" in your life and career that make you feel successful.

Question 130. How Do You Set the Expectations When You Measure Your Progress?

Measurement is the best way to ensure that every dollar used is well spent. When you work with executives, you have to set the campaign expectations in the beginning and give them the benchmarks and measurement to properly gauge success along the way.

Measurement is a two-part equation.

Part I: First comes the definition of exactly what you want to achieve. Too many times, the PR and marketing pros and the executive team are not on the same page when it comes to the expected outcome of a communications program. Right from the start, you need to make sure your goals and objectives are clearly defined not only for your team, but also for your executives.

Part II: The second part comes down to the way you set up your measurement program. I have seen campaigns fall short on the measurement side far too often. PR teams take the time to define goals and objectives. However, they don't have the means to measure or a way to easily track how their efforts reveal they are reaching their goals. Without the proper measurement tools in place, you can't show your progress and benchmark what you've achieved. Measurement, and the tools you need to capture metrics, should be set in place during the planning process and prior to the launch of your campaign.

Always be prepared to discuss measurement details before the rollout of your program, keeping in mind there is a two-part equation. A word to the wise: Don't bother communicating if you can't set the expectations and then measure your outreach. You always have to be prepared to report back on your progress.

Question 131. Can You Define Proof of a Job Well Done?

A gratifying part of your role as a communicator comes from experiencing the tangible results. In PR, the tangibles were always the media placements, customer endorsements, and the positive public opinion that builds over time. However, all these important tangibles take time. For instance, thinking that you can create great exposure right away or building instant credibility to attract new

Figure 6.1 Proof of a Job Well Done

partners and influencers is not easy, and usually doesn't happen overnight. There are, on occasion, those great success stories that happen instantaneously, but they are more of an exception and not necessarily the norm.

What is your proof of a job well done? It is all in the results rolled up together over time, including:

1. large amounts of media coverage;
2. fewer customer complaints;
3. greater brand awareness;
4. motivated and productive employees;
5. happier company stakeholders and a public that is confident in your brand;
6. in the case of a public company, an elevated stock price.

Any, or all, of the above will demonstrate your value and excellent work. You have to be patient and teach others to do the same. There will always be quick PR success, but investing over time will show a job well done and the greatest organizational value.

Question 132. Should Accountability be Across the Board?

Modern communicators have to take accountability to a higher level. What is the best kind of accountability? The accountability executives love to see is tied directly to the company's bottom line. However, you know that is not always possible. What is the Return on Investment (ROI) of a piece of media coverage? Remember, the

Advertising Value Equivalency (AVE) is not a valid measure or acceptable practice. How about the value of a new partnership or a relationship that strengthens over time?

Measurement continues to morph as the media changes. However, the good news … executives also want to see communication impact in the form of customer satisfaction, which could be tied to positive sentiment and testimonials, editorial coverage across different media (including social media), reputation maintenance, greater brand awareness, and how powerful brand messages resonate. These are all important pieces of the ROI puzzle, but may not be seen as immediate tangibles.

Over the years, I have learned to tie PR to the bottom line, as much as possible, to capture executive attention. However, when there is no direct connection, then you have to tie the results you have to other areas within the company working toward similar goals. Marketing, sales, PR, and customer service all work together. The big take away here is that you can't work in a vacuum or silo. Your accountability should be a part of a larger team effort.

You may not be able to immediately pinpoint the ROI of great relationships, but you can show how your communication outreach moved the needle from the people talking about your news, to the traffic you drive to your company's website, to the actions that ensue from there. Being a part of the puzzle is important; your piece counts. However, it is your job to make sure you are sharing your results with the rest of the team. You just might be the missing piece that completes the puzzle picture.

Question 133. Why Is It Important to Explore Big Data?

Understanding data and analytics goes far beyond the research methods I used when first starting out in my career. Today's modern communicators have the opportunity to cross the tech chasm, learning how to dig into data that helps you analyze market trends, better understand audiences, develop more creative pitches, and tie different sets of data together to see a bigger business picture. The results of a communication program should be factored into the higher-level organizational outcomes achieved, by looking at data beyond the PR and communications department. Your data, along with sales, marketing, Web, and customer service, all help to build a more complete picture of business outcomes.

Having access to Big Data or the large amounts of data you own and can use for various purposes is now a part of the PR wheelhouse. Companies will always need professionals in every department who can analyze and report on the data as it relates to their functions. The communications department is no different. The key is for professionals to understand the numbers and gather important insights for smarter communication. Big data is here to stay and communicators need to explore and then embrace how to manage, filter, and use this data daily.[1]

However, having access to data and analytics goes beyond tracking ROI. In communications, we are often focused on proving value rather than improving communication by analyzing data trends. When I interviewed Allyson Hugley, President of Weber Shandwick's Measurement and Analytics Practice, she stressed that good measurement includes understanding data to make better decisions. We will always work to prove our value, but we can also make a big difference and raise the PR bar by showing how we analyze data that leads to sound decision-making for the organization.

Question 134. When It Comes to Big Data ... Is It Quality or Quantity?

Have you ever heard your colleagues talk about how you should not work harder but you should be working smarter? There is truth to this statement. You can spend hours spinning your wheels and wracking your brains on a project to create a lot of "stuff," but not move forward with a more quality output and greater impact.

The same applies when it comes to big data that you can access and how to handle this data. If you apply the quality vs quantity principle, then you don't need big data, more data, or an overabundance of data. On the contrary, you need the right data, which means you have a controlled amount you can filter, manage, and analyze to discover better ways to communicate with your constituents. Things that are bigger are not necessarily better. Bigger can lead to overwhelming amounts of information that do not guide communication but often create confusion. The right data is captured, segmented, and analyzed to guide your outreach.

Having the right data, not big data, and your keen insights will be your best approach to measurement and quality communication.

Question 135. Are You a PR Engineer?

There is a new title for communicators and it is creating a bit of a stir. The title varies from engineer to analytics engineer. These engineers in PR and marketing are being groomed with new skills. Suddenly, having an education in STEM (Science, Technology, Engineering and Math) fields has new importance. For example, the PR analytics engineer is skilled in data capture, filtering information, analyzing the numbers, and formulating the insights to develop stronger relationships and become a more strategic storyteller.

We've been saying (and practicing) for years how PR is both an art and a science. The science part of the role is becoming front and center as technology advances and data becomes more abundant and accessible.

A PR colleague, Leta Soza, Director of PR Engineering and Operations at AirPR, shared her thoughts on the role of the PR engineer. According to Leta, with an internal focus on the brand, the PR engineer has the following responsibilities:

1. analyzes all outgoing communications (earned, owned, bought) to ensure that messages are aligned with the organization's business objectives;
2. develops a deep understanding of the market and customer needs using data;
3. applies analytic aptitude to spot patterns and develops market-based product strategies based on those patterns;
4. looks at internal data and applies it to optimize around how and where the company tells its story;
5. creates and circulates relevant, educational content;
6. develops customer relationships and builds community;
7. becomes a brand champion capable of speaking to core competencies, ethos, and the innovative solutions offered;
8. exercises design skills applicable to social content, marketing collateral, and business development tools;
9. contributes to product innovation.

Are you focused on the science part of communication and how will you make data and analytics a part of your daily function? Are you committed to balancing art and science? When you make data analytics a core part of your function it will not only lead to better storytelling, but also help you to measure your communications success.

Figure 6.2 The PR Engineer

Question 136. How Do You Select the Right Measurement Tools?

Social media has opened up a new toolbox with incredible resources to track, engage, and measure the effect of your communications. Suddenly, proper tool selection becomes an important part of your success. When selecting the tools to gather and filter data from your social media communication, you need to look for the resources that help you to easily report on your progress as you pursue your goals.

The first question to ask is whether your tools help you to achieve your goals. Will your resources track your exposure, engagement, audience preference, advocacy, or some kind of business impact? Other important questions to ask include:

- Will the research tool collect data on a particular social media community for a narrow, more targeted view of your audience? Or, will it capture data across a wide swath of channels for a broader view?
- Is sentiment analysis or emotional analytics available so that you can track how customers feel about your brand?
- Is there the ability to capture your brand's share of brand voice, share of conversation, or even your daily volume of mentions compared to your competitors?
- What are your budgetary constraints? Do you have a budget for paid tools?
- What type of human resources will you need to manage the technology?
- Is any training available for your staff and who will help to get you "up and running" with your tool or technology platform?

- What type of customer service package is available?
- Can you upload your own data into your platform to compare data from other sources?
- Is your resource compatible with other resources you are using for your website tracking tool or CRM software?

These are all important points to evaluate when you are embarking on data collection and then using the information gleaned to draw insights. Most of all, your tools are as good as the source that supports them. You always have to trust your source. You can only be as accurate as the source that feeds you information. Make sure you also take the time to test or trial a measurement platform and spend some time with the customer service team, asking them all your questions. The time they spend with you is a good indication of how they will treat you should you become a customer.

Question 137. Is Your Success Tied to the *Important* Questions?

What are today's organizational challenges and are you still answering those important questions that keep the executives up at night? There are areas of focus that deserve more attention and go beyond tracking your communication goals. Although it is extremely important to prove your ROI, here are some questions that keep PR people at the strategy table because they are helping to improve communications:

- What are you doing to help your company understand audience preferences and their purchasing behavior?
- How is your communication contributing to a larger marketing conversation with various stakeholders?
- How is your communication making your company smarter with respect to what is gaining traction with media?
- Are you informing your company what communication is resonating with the public at large?
- Is the public looking for solutions and are you informing your company there are additional products or services they need to deliver?
- How do you help to improve and drive the business forward?
- What can you do to be less of a cost center and more of a profit center for your company?

Figure 6.3 Success and the Important Questions

It is these important business questions that require you to challenge yourself; to expand your skills and knowledge to answer these questions for your organization. When you can answer the important questions, you begin to take on new roles and responsibilities. Suddenly, you become a communications problem solver across the organization. For me, success and handling the "important" questions go hand in hand.

Question 138. What and How Often Should You Measure to Establish Trends?

If you have nailed down your goals and objectives, know your budget, and have considered your resources, then it is time to put that great measurement program into place. Today, you have an incredible amount of data that can demonstrate how communication drives value. Having a measurement program in place captures the right data—which may include referral traffic, website behavior and performance analytics, share of brand voice, and share of conversation— and will show how your PR is more than just publicity and news coverage. We have advanced far beyond the days of being solely recognized as the folks who write the news releases.

Your efforts drive actions, decisions, and outcomes. However, the trick is always knowing what to measure and how often to spot trends. According to a Nasdaq Chief Communications Officer (CCO) survey in 2016, most corporate communicators are measuring three to four KPIs (Key Performance Indicators). Among the top KPIs most frequently measured were customer lead conversions and brand awareness. At the same time, the survey also revealed that many of the CCOs were measuring more frequently but also swapping in and out different KPIs on a quarterly basis: This accounted for about 44 percent of the respondents. Another 25 percent said that they changed their KPIs monthly. Here's the concern with the frequently changing KPIs ... you're unable to establish a trend if you're switching your measurement. It is always great to explore different metrics, but this should not become a part of your measurement dashboard that you use to report to your company stakeholders or your executive team. When you are establishing the signals that will drive your business, then consistency is really important.[2]

Now ask yourself, "Are you measuring and reporting the right KPIs? Is your measurement dashboard giving you the signals that will help to make the business grow and make your customers happy?" Knowing what and how often to measure with information that empowers the C-Suite is a sure way to get recognized for your accountability and to prove your PR value.

Question 139. What Is the Difference between Strategy and Tactics?

One of the first questions a strategist asks is, "What are our communication goals and how will they tie to higher level business objectives?" Then, depending on your goals you'll ask other questions. "Will our programs raise awareness to help optimize a marketing program or to drive sales?" or "How will managing reputation and preventing crisis maintain the health of our brand over time?" Or, perhaps the PR efforts drive customer satisfaction, or employee productivity. Knowing how to align your programs to higher-level goals is the key to getting attention and trust from the C-Suite.

Thinking like a strategist is focusing on your approach. If you don't think about the approach first, or your strategic direction, then how will you move forward to reach your goals? There is no need to begin the tactical types of communication when they don't support your underlying strategy.

Years ago, I created a YouTube video for my students. It was an example of the difference between goals, objectives, strategies, and tactics.

Here is the example I shared with them:

I have a goal: "I want to lose weight this year."

My objective is, "I'm going to lose x pounds in x # of months." Objectives always have to be quantified and benchmarked over time.

I'm going to achieve my goals and objectives (this is my strategy), by creating a friends group called the "Get Fit Together Program" so we all look and feel great.

These are my communication tactics to get friends to join my new program:

- *Tactic 1:* Email friends an invitation to join the Get Fit Together Program.
- *Tactic 2:* Create and share an online poster with a calendar of activities every month.
- *Tactic 3:* Build a Facebook group where we can discuss activities, share photos, and swap healthy recipes.
- *Tactic 4:* Develop a series of blog posts to highlight activities and group progress.

Remember, creating blog posts, emails, posters, news releases, infographics, eBooks, etc., are communications tactics. If you don't know your approach and you can't envision the goal and evaluate the outcomes, then the tactics just become a lot of stuff you are doing to keep busy.

When you put the goals and strategy first, the tactics will help to drive the actions and support the objectives you want to achieve.

Question 140. How Do You Chart Your Course to the Bigger Picture Finish Line?

You may have small goals you prioritize and reach every day. But there are also those bigger picture goals that require much more of your time, energy, and focus. To visualize big-picture success you have to chart your journey, getting from Point A to Point B, knowing what you are trying to achieve every step of the way. Visualize the bigger picture first, and then document all the steps in between.

You can talk about your bigger goals for years and nothing new will happen. Or, you can make those bigger goals real by actually charting your own course. It is the difference between daily or weekly process goals vs bigger long-term goals that you really can't control. For example, maybe you want to be a famous author or speaker. There are a lot of process or performance goals you can reach on your journey to becoming world renowned.

Creating a roadmap will serve as a guide, as you reach different benchmarks, and evaluate the systems and support to keep you targeted and on course. Remember, the map may change slightly along the way. For example, when you put together an itinerary for a trip, there may be airline changes and some activities may shift depending on the weather. You may have to adjust your plans to accommodate your travel companions, and other fine-tuning, as you move along.

For the bigger picture, stating your goals out loud vs the exercise of mapping to visualize the steps to your goals are two very different approaches. The latter helps you envision your course, making it more realistic and laser-focused. As a result, every time you reach a new benchmark (a performance goal) your drive to the finish line will become stronger.

Don't just say it ... map it out and do it.

Question 141. What Is Your Definition of Success?

What looked like success at age 20, 30, or even 40 is not my definition of success today. By all means, it is not supposed to be. During my younger years in PR, my success was working in an agency and securing top tier media for my clients. My mentor told me that if I could get my clients into the *Wall Street Journal*, *The New York Times*, and on *Good Morning America*, then this would be great success for a young professional.

For years, I remember striving for media pitching success. But my goals soon changed. I entered into a new phase of business and life. With a young daughter, success was making sure I could provide for her at the time and for her future. I started my own business and wanted to build up an agency that would be recognized nationally with big name brands as clients. Of course, securing the great media coverage was still a part of the success of my business, but it took a back seat. Other members of my team jumped in to do the pitching, while I invested my time in new business pitches and negotiating contracts.

Once again, the picture of success changed after becoming an author and then transitioning into the communications consultant role I play today. Every phase of my life changed my outlook on success. Today, I'm focused on successful problem solving for my consulting clients, training teams to embrace the changing media landscape, writing books to help students and professionals, which also includes my new media initiatives, podcasting, and being a LinkedIn Learning Instructor video author.

I'm not sure if it was a conscious effort or a higher power guiding me, but the twists and turns of fate shaped my personal and professional success at every phase. When it comes to your success, my advice is to always trust your instincts and the very smart people who support you. My inner circle of colleagues and friends have always been a good gut check when embarking on big new ventures.

Of course, your career and measuring your own success will equate to how you prioritize your goals and what you feel is most important to you and the significant people in your life. When your picture of success changes, let it happen; these are the signs that you are growing and advancing in your career and life.

Question 142. Is the Advertising Value Equivalency (AVE) a Useful Measure?

If you're in PR … here's a simple answer. No. In the past, PR agencies and professionals relied on AVEs, or the Advertising Value Equivalency, as a way to show earned media coverage value. I was guilty back in the day of using this measure for our clients too. It was so easy to say to a VP of communications or a C-Level executive, "If you had to pay for this type of coverage in *The New York Times* or the *Wall Street Journal*, in terms of paid advertising space, then the ad dollars would have cost you $X." The AVE was used to show what your editorial coverage was worth in terms of advertising column inches. This little statement, with this valueless equivalent, made executives really happy.

Well, this is no longer the way to measure and now it is time to educate executives and manage their PR earned media coverage expectations a different way. Just because you like something does not mean it is good for you or it will really help you to see an accurate picture in the long run. What is interesting to note is the AVE is still a preferred measure. The Nasdaq CCO measurement survey revealed that the AVE was among the top KPIs being measured by CCO survey participants. It came in third, next to customer lead conversion (what percentage of customer leads convert to sales) and brand awareness/consideration (the extent that people are able to recognize and consider your brand), which are considered really important measures.

The Barcelona Principles, developed in 2010, clearly stated that we needed standard measurement and it was not going to be the AVE. The principles also outlined how we had to budget for measurement, talk the language of business, and basically adopt a new measurement mindset.[3] The Barcelona Principles were updated again in 2015, and nothing changed with respect to AVEs. They were just as "taboo" then as they were back in 2010.

Clearly, modern communicators have to find a better approach and get rid of the past measures that do not meet today's measurement standards. What can you rely on to measure your PR? Traffic to your website, engagement and performance analytics, customer lead conversion, brand message awareness and message pull through, and search engine traffic.

Embrace a new day and don't fall into an old measurement trap. Educate your executives on useful and better KPIs. Show them the real value and you'll find yourself branded as a trusted modern communicator.

The Experts Weigh In

Shonali Burke, CEO of Shonali Burke Consulting

Learn Practical Measurement

It's a little astounding to me that, for all the advances we have made as an industry, our measurement practices are still largely stuck in the Dark Ages.

We keep talking about "the seat at the table," but we refuse to learn, and speak, the language of business. And the language of business is about revenue and the bottom-line. If we, as PR strategists, counselors, and practitioners, cannot communicate our value in these terms, we will never get that seat at the table, because we just don't deserve it.

I've been interested in measurement as far back as I can remember. It's exciting to me; frankly, there's nothing like that high, knowing that what you did made a difference. So regardless of whether I was still in the agency world, or in-house, I always wanted to know how we could prove PR's value.

These days, there are so many resources on smart measurement and analytics, there is really no excuse for not educating one's self. You don't have to be a statistician to be able to measure smartly. You simply have to think like the strategic thinker you are, and work backwards from your goal. *That* is the best way to set up smart and practical measurement frameworks.

For example, when we designed and implemented the Blue Key Campaign for USA for UNHCR, we knew exactly how many key purchases we were working towards. But we also knew that key purchases by themselves were only the means to an end; to build a really engaged community that could help share the organization's story, with the ultimate goal of growing their member base.

So we certainly measured key purchases, but we also looked at how many Blue Key Champions we secured. We looked at how many of them started participating in the digital events we'd organize, such as the tweetathons, and we tracked how the conversation in different platforms converted in terms of website visits.

When we saw a particular tactic working, we'd do more of it. If something wasn't working, we'd refocus the strategy around what did work. But we wouldn't have been able to do any of this if a) we weren't looking at the analytics on a regular basis, and b) we weren't keeping our eyes focused on the ultimate goal.

How many impressions did we generate? I have no idea. Sure, we have reports that detail the potential reach of Twitter chats, and so on. But at the end of the day, we measured what mattered, and what could make a difference to the organization, and its efforts to help refugees.

That is practical measurement.

Rebekah Iliff, Chief Strategy Officer, AirPR

Beware of Vanity Metrics, Go for Value-Driven

Vanity, to any degree, is typically a substitute for things (or people) that lack true substance. In our modern, self-obsessed culture, we all suffer from some level of vanity—but beyond a certain threshold, it shifts from tolerable to destructive.

For years, the PR industry in aggregate has struggled to prove its value, lagging behind technological innovation—at least from a quantitative standpoint. The very fact that PR exists and commands budgets is difficult for many to wrap their heads around; therefore, even proponents of PR often meet it with suspicion and skepticism. As a result, the industry has been somewhat forced to create arbitrary, often "inflated" metrics in order to get a seat at the proverbial table.

As PR practitioners now living in an era of analytics, insights, and structured data, it should be our number one priority to rid ourselves, our agencies, and our brands of vanity metrics and move toward value-driven metrics that showcase not only what's working to move the needle; but also what's not working so we can create better strategies and tactical approaches that ultimately map to business outcomes.

Vanity 1. Impressions: I'm sorry to be the bearer of bad fantasy-land news, but in the world of PR, 5 billion eyeballs scanning a headline of your very sexy press release doesn't actually have any measurable impact. It's a nice-big-fat-juicy-number, but it will not map to insights about your PR activities; and it will not enable you to make better decisions about the brand you represent.

What to measure: Map traffic to your website *directly attributed* to PR activities. It will be a much lower number than the "impression" number, but will give you a more accurate depiction of your key audience segments' interest in your brand.

Vanity 2. Hits: As one of my favorite PR measurement gurus, Katie Delahaye Paine, so aptly states: "HITS are How Idiots Track Success." Media placements are the result of extremely hard work, to be sure—but are not an end in and of themselves.

What to measure: Observe how the audience is engaging with the media placement and whether or not it drives them to take any specific interactions on your digital properties: Social shares, blog sign ups, whitepaper downloads, demo requests.

Vanity 3. Share of voice: "Share of Voice" (the percentage of all online content and conversations about your company, compared against those of your competitors), is a term I hear regularly in meetings with CMOs (Chief Marketing Officers) during discussions of success metrics.

The caveat of using Share of Voice as a proxy for PR measurement?

For starters, it's impossible to manually track all of the online content and conversations without sophisticated machine learning, data mining, and natural language processing (NLP) technology. So, what you're left with is likely 25–30 percent accuracy around those results when it comes to what really moves the needle for your business.

Second, going back to this idea of vanity, it matters less how much share of the industry voice you have, and more about the quality of the voice and whether or not your key constituents actually understand what it is you have to say.

What to measure: Track the key messages for your brand and see how the media are placing them in news articles, blog posts, etc. Then, continue to track these key messages across social channels to understand which ones are resonating or "sticking" with core audience segments: The ones who will actually buy your products or services. This is what I like to call "Power of Voice."

The Future of Value-driven Measurement: Even the most sophisticated companies give weight to different aspects of their PR efforts. PR will never be a "one size fits all" solution. By nature, it requires a creative process and extreme level of influence in order to have an impact.

But measurement for measurement's sake will have little impact on PR's future as a key driver of business. In fact, it will most likely have the adverse effect. Doing away with vanity metrics—which lack substance and serve to perpetuate the idea that you can't measure PR activities with any real accuracy—is the first step toward creating a viable framework for PR measurement.

Heather Whaling, CEO, Geben Communication

Define Your All

We grow up being told what it means to be a good son or daughter, mother or father, husband or wife, friend, employee, or boss. It's impossible to excel at everything, which is why we often feel like we can't have it all.

When I was pregnant, people often asked when I'd slow down or how I'd ever balance motherhood with entrepreneurship. It made me hyper-aware of the pressure to live up to society's expectations of a career woman *and* a mom.

In the two years since having my son, my company has grown from four employees to more than 20, plus we've expanded our geographic footprint. Despite being a fast-growing business, I still manage to leave the office three days a week at 4.00 p.m. to spend quality time with him. I hang out with him every morning before heading to work—even if it's just reading one book or chatting while getting ready for the day.

I'm not the stereotypical "Pinterest mom." I'm not crafty. I'm barely organized enough to put up Christmas decorations. Decorating for Valentine's Day, St. Patrick's Day, or Easter is out of the question. While I love cooking dinner, I've never mastered baking, so I order cake for my son's birthday.

But, my kid is smart, curious, loving, and happy. My company is growing. I'm creating jobs for talented, kind people, and we're doing work that matters.

It's not about being a career woman *or* a stay-at-home-mom. It's not either/or. It's and. It's about finding satisfaction, personally *and* professionally. People can, in fact, achieve ambitious careers goals *and* be good parents. Of course, it takes a village, but it's doable.

Can you have it all? Absolutely, but first you need to get crystal clear on *your* priorities. Define *your* all. Don't let anyone else define success for you.

Sandra Fathi, President AFFECT

On Measuring Your Success

It has been my experience that public relations professionals have a real sense of fear when it comes to measurement. It's not clear to me why, or how, this fear became so ingrained in the PR practice, but when you look at other professions there doesn't seem to be nearly as much anxiety around this issue. Let's take accountants for example. Are they afraid to find out how much revenue the company earned? Or, how much profit? What about an athlete? Would he or she be afraid to find out their time for running a marathon? Probably not.

PR professionals seem to have mastered the art of avoiding measurement or measuring things that aren't actually any measure of success. When clients first come to an agency, they talk about things like improving a company's reputation or increasing awareness of products and services they offer. In some cases, they may be more specific, like increase sales among Millennials in the New York market. When we think about these goals objectively and ask ourselves how would we measure their success, it certainly would not be through ad equivalency or number of articles let alone the number of tweets or likes on a post. Yet those measurements seem to be in our comfort zone. We need to get out of our comfort zone and measure what matters—and what is a true indicator of meeting those objectives.

Improving a company's reputation might be measured by a survey—before and after a PR campaign—to see if public opinion has improved. Alternatively, we might look at sentiment on social media or in media coverage as compared to the prior period. If we were trying to increase awareness of a particular product, then it would be helpful to know how many people heard or read about the product. However, we need real, tangible numbers—and not some of the theoretical algorithms that estimate "reach"' based on the number of Twitter followers or Facebook friends someone has, since most of us are not staring at our feeds 24/7. Let's look at things the executive team understands and values—how many people are visiting the website, downloading information, signing up for events, joining a mailing list, buying products, and recommending us to others? We just need to trace where they came from—did they read that *New York Times* article? Did they follow a link from LinkedIn? Did they hear the CEO speak at that conference? All of those PR activities helped lead to an action that the organization values and demonstrate progress towards reaching business goals.

Public relations professionals need to understand how measurement helps us—if we know how our programs are currently performing, we can invest more in efforts that have the most positive results and abandon those that don't seem to be providing any tangible benefit. Wouldn't it be great to do less work if we find out that some of the things we are tasked with aren't contributing to the company's mission? And, wouldn't it be wonderful to focus on the activities that make a meaningful contribution to the company instead?

Notes

1 Microsoft website, "What is Big Data?" March 2017. Available at: https://msdn.microsoft.com/en-us/library/dn749868.aspx (accessed May 17, 2017).
2 Nasdaq Corporate Solutions and KRC Research, Chief Communications Officer Measurement Survey, March 2017.
3 Andrea Manning and David Rockland, Ph.D., The Public Relations Strategist, Understanding the Barcelona Principles, March 21, 2011. Available at: http://apps.prsa.org/Intelligence/TheStrategist/Articles/view/9072/1028/Understanding_the_Barcelona_Principles#.WSn15xPysXo (accessed May 17, 2017).

Chapter 7

Giving Back as a Mentor

Mentoring is a fundamental part of your personal development and career growth, whether you are first starting out or you are a veteran in your industry. I started mentoring employees and colleagues in communications about 20 years ago and I still have mentors I rely on today. What always amazes me the most about mentoring is you are never too inexperienced or seasoned to ask for help. For example, I received a note from two students in middle school who attended Ecole Bilingue de Berkeley in California. They wanted an expert to help with their National History Day (NHD) project by answering a few questions. Obviously, they had learned at a young age if you don't know an answer, find a professional to help you.

Mentoring is a gift which should not be taken for granted, whether you are the mentor or the mentee. Regardless of your role, it is a great feeling to be a part of a two-way learning process. I've relied on my mentors for years. My mentor was there to help me find my first job in public relations and then more than 20 years later, he made an introduction for me that led to a teaching assignment at a university. I've had other mentors over the years who have come in and out of my career. What often makes me smile is that many professionals probably don't even realize that they are mentoring, just by sharing information freely. I guess that is more of a reason for you to let them know and to thank them for their support and guidance over the years.

You will find that as you navigate your career, you and your mentor can form a very close relationship. Or, you can learn just by watching professionals you admire. Social media really helps you to find professionals who openly share advice, offer insights, and discuss their career experiences daily. Take what you learn from them, be thankful, and pay it forward.

But, how do you know when it is time to become a mentor? What role will you play in mentoring your younger peers? No one will ever come right out and say to you, "Okay, now, you had better begin mentoring your peers." With the demanding pressures of the modern communicator's lifestyle, no one is really keeping tabs on you. You have to be the one to always sharpen your own skills (get mentored) and then apply what you have learned to become a mentor. Of course, some professionals have a natural gift and it is their unspoken actions that demonstrate their natural knack for mentoring, without ever having to pursue a mentee.

The questions and answers in this chapter will help you to decide when it is time to mentor so you can share the stories/lessons you feel are valuable, when you decide it is time. At some point in your career, you'll want to give back. There is a point when the principles and experiences that have influenced you over the years will help someone else. The Q&A in this chapter are all the most frequently asked questions from my mentees over the years in an effort to understand the best ways to approach their career growth. What I quickly learned from mentoring is that with every experience, you'll also learn very quickly; it is a reverse mentoring process. You can share advice and learn a lot at the same time.

Question 143. Do You Still Feel "Butterflies" in Your Stomach?

Consider yourself lucky if you have the same rush of adrenalin or nervous, excited feeling every time you make a new business presentation, pitch a story to the media, build a relationship with a partner, or negotiate a contract. When you feel the excitement on a daily basis, this is a good sign that you truly enjoy what you do.

The "butterflies" in your stomach are not negative. They are positive energy. You are, indeed, fortunate if you can go down your career path feeling the thrill of every communication, as an intern, an entry-level employee, or during the later phases of your profession.

For me, the butterflies still come on fast and furious; for example, right before an important media interview. I remember a broadcast interview at NBC in Connecticut. I was ready with my talking points and the host of the show had already shared the news clips we would be discussing from the evening before. But, when the segment began, I felt that surge of energy. The butterflies were definitely flying around. The same occurs when I'm on stage presenting to an audience. They also appear as I walk into a new business meeting and when I host industry events. The butterflies represent my enthusiasm and spirit; they are sensations that make me feel great about what I do and why I work long hours in a day.

However, if you can't find the butterflies, or they are replaced with an uneasiness in your stomach, then you have to recognize this too. When I interviewed Jane Boyce, President of Tru Vue, she was very candid about what you need to do if a sick feeling comes over you when you are driving to work. She said, "If two out of ten days you feel sick to your stomach, then you may want to explore some new opportunities." You have to distinguish between the excited butterflies and the uneasy and unpleasant feelings you are experiencing.[1]

My best advice is to get in tune with those butterflies. Make a mental note when they appear. When you feel the butterflies, they are a good indication you have found your true passion. Let them reinforce your decision to forge ahead in your career.

Question 144. What Does It Take to Get to the Top?

When you are assigned a role, cutting the corners may seem like the quick way to get your work done and advance to the next level. However, sometimes we take the more administrative type of tasks for granted. I've been asked by younger professionals, "Why do we have to learn these smaller tasks?" It is extremely important to gain knowledge of the tasks that help to fine-tune your skills. For example, when you are in communications, you may start out with a set number of tasks before you move to more involved strategic planning and development of your company's marketing programs.

As a younger professional you can expect to be involved in:

- researching media, the market, and the competition;
- uncovering journalist and blogger pitching preferences;
- building targeted media lists for different campaigns and events;
- learning various types of writing styles for different content formats;
- tracking and monitoring keywords through social media to uncover important conversations;
- reporting on news coverage and keeping a close eye on audience sentiment about your communication;
- actively engaging your brand's community members on social media;
- pitching the media through a number of different channels;
- assisting with events and client initiatives;
- wearing different hats to help your team to be successful.

Now this does not mean that you won't be involved in other activities, which is the wearing different hats part. But the more details you know starting out, the better off you will be when you manage your own team of professionals someday. Be the sponge that soaks up all of the learning and is then able to teach someone else. How do you ask people to perform tasks that you cannot properly explain or do yourself? Cutting corners may mean you skip the hands-on experience that helps you to direct others to do the same.

When you are moving your way up the chain of command, don't cut the corners, no matter what position you hold. Be the professional who always masters the process, knows the best approach, and has a deeper understanding of what your team or your company is trying to achieve.

Question 145. Why Is It Important to be a #ForeverStudent?

There is no pretending you are an expert, if you have not been exposed to the proper training, mentoring, or experiences. However, today, your education does not have to be confined to the traditional learning environment. You can find courses online, and you will also find dynamic discussion in social media communities, where you can learn from professionals who are more than willing to share information.

People learn in different ways. You may get your undergraduate or graduate degree and then continue your education with industry certifications. Some professionals choose to increase their knowledge through online resources such as Massive Open Online Courses (MOOCs). Or, you may prefer a hands on apprenticeship. Regardless of the method of learning, you always have to stay connected to your industry and the professionals who will guide you as mentors or sponsors. Ask yourself, "Would you want a doctor or lawyer who didn't have ongoing learning experiences in their field, and stopped their continuing education?"

I remember a Twitter conversation with a fellow colleague. I had read her LinkedIn post about her quest for continued learning. I reached out to tell her that I appreciated her post and that I was a #ForeverStudent. She said, "What a perfect hashtag, I'd join that group." She then followed up by asking the topics we were going to discuss in a #ForeverStudent Twitter chat. Of course, it was just a concept in my mind, but it proves that there are professionals similar to myself who are actively in this #ForeverStudent club.

Figure 7.1 The #Forever Student Club
Adapted from Twitter

The #ForeverStudent has an ongoing passion for learning. The #ForeverStudent will not stop where the physical classroom ends.

Question 146. Why Should You Go Where the Professionals Go?

Going where the professionals go means active involvement with your state or national industry groups. For example, I started as a member of the Public Relations Student Society of America (PRSSA) in college, and then transitioned to the Public Relations Society of America (PRSA) as I entered into the PR profession. Today, I'm a member of the New Jersey chapter and the national association.

You should take advantage of the resources and the networking opportunities these types of industry organizations provide, both online and in-person at events. Networking is a must for any professional in every industry. Networking and creating long-lasting connections can lead to mentors, business opportunities, new positions, and up-to-date information from professionals who know their business and are more than willing to share their expertise.

Joining an association helps you to:

- have access to new learning opportunities, seminars, conferences, and professional development;
- network with professionals that you would not normally have direct access to through an organization's website or their online directory;
- find partnering organizations that may help you with your projects and initiatives if they have complementary services;
- learn from top professionals in your industry;
- be a part of a credible organization to raise your own industry profile;
- give back to your profession when you join as a member or as a volunteer.

A professional association helps you to be closer to the professionals in your industry. However, you should still be networking through social media and using your established connections to excel in your career. Making it your goal to find an association will give you that extra edge on learning and the latest news and information in your industry.

Modern communicators are in a race for relevance and the benefits of an association with a professional support system can help you to stand out in your field.

Question 147. How Do You Know If You Are Ready to Mentor?

You may be 20+ years in communications. Or, maybe you are a three- to five-year member of the profession. Can it ever be too early to mentor a more junior professional? There are different schools of thought on the topic. Some professionals feel that you have to be a certain number of years in the profession to offer sound advice. However, due to the nature of technology and the way we are connecting and learning, I offer a different type of mentoring test.

Figure 7.2 The Right Time to Mentor

Here are a few questions and accomplishments to consider as a way to help you decide when it is time for you to mentor.

1. Is your work contribution being recognized as instrumental to your organization or your industry? If you are working on new initiatives and receiving accolades for your work, then it may be time to pass along some of your extensive knowledge.
2. Have you been asked to speak at industry association events, local or regional programs in your industry, or speaking engagements on a broader scale to share your expertise? When you're asked to speak on different topics to share your expertise, then you are ready for mentoring.
3. Do you lead a team of professionals? When you are leading a team and helping them to navigate various initiatives under your direction, then it is time to mentor.
4. Do you find yourself naturally helping younger professionals? When younger professionals look like they need help and you feel you have the answers to share, then you are ready to mentor.

Take a good look at yourself, and what you do. Then, take the time to identify the needs of professionals around you. Is there a younger pro or a peer who needs help, but who may be too nervous to ask you? Do you possess knowledge and a skill to help someone along their career path? Giving back as a mentor sometimes means initiating the assistance before you're asked.

Mentors are being groomed every day, but no one is there to tell them it is time to become a mentor. You have to realize it on your own and just start paying it forward, taking the time to share all of the best practices you have learned.

Did you know every January is recognized as National Mentoring Month? Maybe it is time to either thank a mentor or gear up to become one at the beginning of the new year.

Question 148. What Skills Do You Need to Get Noticed?

Today, a modern communicator has to be more than just a good writer and relationship builder. I am frequently asked, "What are the skills that employers look for in PR and communication new hires?" Here is a good starting list:

- proficiency in new technologies including social media, mobile, etc.;
- strategic thinkers who can see and understand the bigger business picture;
- detailed oriented implementers who can deliver on time and under budget;
- good negotiators who can liaise between friendly and contentious groups if necessary;
- great idea generators who are innovative in their thinking;
- strong writers that know how to write for different media channels;
- individuals with high Emotional Quotient (EQ) to handle sensitive situations;
- professionals with logical/analytical thought processes;
- data savviness: understanding how to capture, analyze, and use data to make better decisions;
- ethical communicators in an age of social conversations;
- professionals with strong interpersonal skills who can build relationships via different media channels;
- confident speakers with stage presence and/or the ability to command a room.

The most successful professionals are able to apply these natural skills to reach communication and business success. How do you rate yourself in these areas and where do you need help?

Question 149. How Do You Prepare for the New Job Interview and Aptitude Test?

Any job interview is easy if you prepare properly. Years ago, these were some of the most frequently asked questions when interviewing for an entry-level position in PR:

- Do you know how to write a news release? (Followed by a written test.)
- Where have you secured editorial coverage, print, broadcast, and online?
- What was your most successful PR campaign and why?
- What are some of the PR obstacles you have encountered dealing with a client, partner, media professional, or another team member?
- Who is the toughest audience that you have ever dealt with and why?
- What are your strengths and your weaknesses as a communicator?
- What is your personal definition of PR?

The above are the more "traditional" PR and marketing questions, and ones I would have used in the past to screen interview, years ago when I owned my marketing communications firm. However, today the questions have changed. Not only will you be asked the "traditional" questions, you may also be tested on your modern communication and creative skills. The newer interview questions reflect what I call a "Hybrid" approach that captures how modern communicators have moved out of their silos, embracing new technologies, analytics, and creative skills.

Several of the questions may look something like this:

- How do you use a mix of media to increase awareness and build credibility?
- Have you ever heard of the PESO model?
- Discuss your writing … what are your digital and social media writing strengths?
- What design tools have you used to build presentations, infographics, memes, and/or reports?
- Are you able to develop a blog in WordPress, or what blog platforms do you know?
- What social media tracking software are you familiar with?

- Give an example of your most creative media pitch?
- How familiar are you with SEO and SEM?
- Have you ever created videos for YouTube or podcasts for iTunes?
- How familiar are you with live streaming video?
- What does branding mean to you?
- And, now for my favorite ... how well is our brand reflected through our social media channels?

These are certainly a different set of questions than what I was asked years ago. With consumer behavior changing, technology advancing and attention spans dwindling, organizations need employees who have more experience with different technologies and a higher Creative Quotient (CQ) with different types of media.

Question 150. What Is the Best Way to Learn about a Career?

A career in communications today is different than when I graduated in the late 1980s. You have to write for different types of media channels, build relationships with various community groups (including online and social), conduct real-time research, get involved in fundraising, work on events both physically and virtually, become a social media manager, handle internal social and collaborative communications, and the list goes on. The world of communications is tied to communication challenges, and crosses many different areas and specialties.

To see if PR and marketing are right for you, talking to many different professionals and learning from their experiences really helps. However, the best way to learn is to shadow a professional for a day. I remember years ago having interns spend the day with me or even a few days to truly experience "a day in the life" of a PR and marketing professional. They were able to attend client meetings, in-person and on the telephone, and participate in brainstorming exercises and strategy meetings. They also assisted on some client projects under close supervision. Of course, clients gave full permission for my shadows to participate and they were happy to have new helpers in meetings and participating in account work.

The experience, in every case, helped to transition an unsure student or young professional into embracing a position and a career more fully. Every time, their decision to pursue communications was validated. When you can open your day and your mind to this experience, your shadow will learn the real meaning of being a modern communicator.

The "thank you" always comes in the form of their choice to pursue a career in your field.

Question 151. How Much Should You Pay Attention to Your Competitive Peers?

For me, competition started at an early age. At the age of 12, I began horse show competitions, participating in events almost every weekend until I about 18 years old. Of course, the spirit of competition carried into my adult life and career, as I was constantly challenging myself to do more and get the most out of every opportunity. However, knowing the rate at which you move and excel is really important. There are times when you may be tempted to look at a colleague who is moving at lightning speed. Remember, their pace is not your pace.

If lightning speed is what you want and you can be as effective and efficient, produce quality work, and feel great about what you have done, then go for it. But if you are making numerous errors and upsetting your normal rhythm of activity, then you may want to re-evaluate your pace, so you can be the best *you* can be. This is all about you, and no one can determine the speed at which you excel. You have to excel at your own pace.

Here is how you can determine a good pace for your learning and professional growth. Ask yourself:

1. Are you reaching the goals you set and discussing them in performance reviews to receive feedback from your supervisor? Is the feedback positive?
2. Do you differentiate between regular goals and big stretch goals you strive to achieve?
3. Does your work stand out and is it being recognized by peers and higher ups in your company?
4. Do you feel challenged (in a good way) with each and every project and initiative you complete?
5. Do you feel you are learning and growing from the people around you?
6. Do you feel you are taking more initiative and seeking out a leadership role when you work in a group?

Figure 7.3 Keeping Your Own Pace

If you can answer these questions and feel good about your responses, then you are learning and growing at a good pace ... your pace.

Remember, your pace has to feel right for you because you always answer to yourself first.

Question 152. Do You Know Your Daily Boundaries?

Similar to Question 39, you have to know when to say, "No." It took me years to learn that "No" is a more powerful word than "Yes." You only have so many hours in a day and the choices you make should always move you toward happy, healthy, and fulfilled. Overworking, finding yourself over-extended, and depleting yourself of every last bit of energy is not good for you or the people around you.

By taking time to find the right daily boundaries (work blended with personal time), you can frequently push the reset button and quickly find your focus with even more creativity. I started to say, "No," to many of the meetings, fundraisers, networking events, sponsorships, and luncheon invitations. Then, when I finally said, "Yes" to select opportunities, I found the events were better suited for me. I was a thoughtful participant in those activities, being able to contribute in a more meaningful way.

Here's a little test to help you establish your own daily boundaries and to really evaluate if every invitation you accept helps or hinders your growth potential. If you answer "Yes" more than twice during this test, then it is time to step back to establish better boundaries for yourself.

1. Are you agreeing to participate in activities because you don't want to hurt someone's feelings?
2. Are you saying "Yes" out of some kind of obligation or guilt?
3. Have you said "Yes" to an invitation because a friend, peer, or colleague would be annoyed if you didn't?
4. Do you say "Yes" to events when your first gut instinct is to immediately say "No"?
5. Do you find yourself saying "Yes" even though your acceptance to the event, meeting, dinner, networking event, etc., is not a top priority?
6. Are you inclined to accept an invitation because you don't know your daily, monthly, and long-term priorities/goals?

Questions like these help you to protect your priorities and keep you balanced and evenly blending your work/life activities; the places where you really need to focus. Whether you are single and on your own, or you are a family person with different home responsibilities, you have to focus on your daily boundaries ... in every phase of your life.

Work with me here. Practice saying "No," and feeling good about your decision; it is for your own benefit. If you say "No" more, then you'll feel a lot better when you decide to say "Yes."

Question 153. Can You Work Hard, Help Others, and Still Focus on Personal Goals?

If you are managing a busy career and family life, then you may find yourself slightly off course with respect to goals and personal growth. What is the first thing to exit your routine when you are actively involved with work, family, and friends? Is it your goal setting and personal development? If you answered "Yes," then it is time to make a date with yourself to refocus on your own ambition and passion.

Remember, it is never too late to move forward to reclaim the time. Start small, with baby steps, just to find a few moments in a day. Here are a few ways to find, and promote, your personal goals, carving out time for you:

1. If you are a morning person, then you should set aside quiet time before the sun comes up. When the house is quiet you can grab your favorite drink and sit quietly with yourself. You will be amazed at how clear your mind will be.

2. If you stay up late at night, then this may be your best time for personal goal planning. Don't just lie in bed trying to fall asleep with thoughts of what you didn't do during the day. Get out of bed and take the time to think about how you can be more productive the next day and what productivity really means to you.
3. Let your loved ones know you need to take a "time out." This is the equivalent of placing a "Meeting in Progress" sign on your door. Don't worry, they'll get used to it. Then take the time to meet with yourself to determine what is important to you.
4. Write down your daily routine and track your actions for a few days in a row. You will be surprised at how much you watch Cable TV news and the political news shows, or how much you search your Instagram for #Beabull and #Beagle puppies. Okay, that is one of my guilty pleasures, but you may have one too.
5. Take a break in your routine and find a new quiet spot for goal setting. Sometimes it is difficult to do this in your living room with the TV on or when your kids are streaming Netflix nearby. Change your setting to help you focus, set goals, and prioritize your action steps.

You can easily get all-consumed with your work, family, and helping others to succeed. However, you must find the time for yourself, building your greater purpose, achieving personal goals, and feeling satisfied. When you do, then you will naturally become an even more thoughtful, giving, and helpful resource to the people around you.

Question 154. Is It Better to be Proactive or Wait to be Asked?

Today, companies are looking for people who will raise their hands and want to get involved. You have to step outside of your own silo and your comfort zone, all on your own. New areas where you can get involved might include completely different departments in your organization where you may be able to lend a helping hand. The rule of thumb: You should not wait for someone to give you the assignment, especially if you identify an area in your department or company that is struggling and needs support.

But, you may be asking yourself, what is the best way to be hands on and how do I find these opportunities to solve problems? Here are a few steps you can take within your own organization to set you on the path to being proactive and getting involved as a problem solver.

1. Talk to people at your company; network beyond your own team.
2. Listen in on company Town Hall meetings, if they are available, to hear what is going on in the company and on a much larger scale.
3. Talk to your HR department about growth opportunities and you will quickly find out the areas that need additional support.
4. Encourage team building and extracurricular activities not only with your team but cross functional teams as well.
5. Participate in company activities, yearly holiday parties, networking events, and give back days. The more you can get out of your silo and learn from others, the more you will hear about the challenges in other areas of the company.
6. When you meet new people in your firm, ask questions about them and their work. Then listen carefully to find out what is going on in their world. Your continued listening and learning helps you to offer solutions and to get involved.

When you expose yourself to different people and open yourself up to new opportunities, you are being proactive. Then, you are able to be a problem solver who can offer assistance and propose new ideas to tackle challenges.

The initiative you take will make you stand out from your peers. Being proactive and involved means taking steps to branch out and not waiting to be asked.

Question 155. How Prepared Are You?

No matter how junior or senior you are in your organization, you must come into a meeting fully prepared. Proper preparation goes far beyond having a pad and pen in hand or your laptop for taking digital notes.

Here is what being prepared means in the business setting:

1. Being prepared involves challenging yourself to think about and answer the questions a supervisor or boss may ask you during the meeting.
2. Understanding your purpose or why you were invited to the meeting in the first place will help you to prepare. If you don't

know why, then ask this question in advance: "Is there something you would like me to cover/discuss during this meeting?"
3. Think about the questions that may be directed to you because of your role or your responsibilities in the organization.
4. Find out who else will be in attendance at the meeting so you know who may ask a question, regarding different topics or issues. Professionals from your company all have different meeting objectives.

Sure, there will be times when you are asked to participate in a meeting, and you may be doing a lot of listening. However, I have learned that if you are in a meeting, then you play a role. Make sure you fully understand that role, and make sure you show up with the right information and the important questions to answer.

Question 156. What Does a Mentor Really Do?

Mentors are there for information, guidance, and to open doors for their mentees. I try not to tell people what to do, but give them ideas and inspiration to come to good conclusions on their own. My mentors have always taken the position of a directional compass and a good gut check system. Here are what you should look for in a mentor:

1. A good educator. A mentor is an individual who not only shares crucial professional development steps but also demonstrates these steps.
2. A door opener. A mentor has a professional network, is more than willing to open doors for you, and helps you to meet other people who may be able to assist in career advancement.
3. A good listener. A mentor knows how to listen and probes more deeply with questions, so their mentees can figure out a situation and come to important conclusions.
4. A support system. A mentor supports and is a guiding beacon. Your mentor should help to inspire, motivate, and work with you to navigate your professional development roadmap.

When I think about my mentors, it has been about learning through their experiences. I would watch, listen, and learn. There are tremendous opportunities when you find a mentor that understands what you are trying to achieve. At the same time, I offer the same for my mentees. Of course, open communication is the key to a successful mentor/mentee relationship. Transparency and open communication lets people know what you need.

Question 157. What Can You Do to Become a Better Role Model?

I remember years ago working with an executive at my old agency. Something had gone terribly wrong in her department and it affected one of our client accounts. I asked what had happened; the answer was surprising. Unfortunately, this particular client error had occurred under her direct watch. Her response to me was, "I don't know the first thing about it. I haven't really been involved."

The executive was being honest, which I appreciated. But, there was a big red flag that immediately popped up in my mind. My executive was not at all familiar with a process in her own department. She was definitely considered a role model at the agency, in so many ways. However, there was an important element missing. Practice what you preach.

When I think about my different roles, I have asked myself a tough question: "Was I truly a role model?" Did I know everything that I had asked my colleagues or employees (depending on my role) to do? Did I have direct hands-on experience or at least a good working knowledge? For the most part, I can say "Yes," especially in the latter part of my career.

Because hindsight is always 20/20, here is my list of tips to become a better role model so you can start right away:

- *Practice what you preach:* It is difficult to ask others to do something if you haven't experienced it yourself. How do you answer questions in depth, share your personal perspective, and inspire others to tackle their challenges? You can't just be saying it ... you have to be doing it or at least fully understand what it is that they are doing.
- *Believe deeply in what you do:* When you believe in what you are doing it truly shows. Others pick up on your deep enthusiasm and excitement. I can't imagine a role model who isn't drinking some kind of Kool Aid!
- *Strive to always be better:* Role models don't just accept the status quo. Absolutely not. They are role models because

they constantly up the ante for themselves and the people around them, so everyone benefits.

- *Dare to be different:* As a role model, it is okay to be different, if different means being true to who you are and what you stand for. Your uniqueness will make you stand out and be appreciated.
- *Be human and show concern:* Just because you are the role model doesn't mean the focus is on you. After all, what is a role model if no one is modeling after you? You have to always show your appreciation, respect, and gratitude. The best role models are caring and go out of their way to help others to benefit.
- *Make mistakes and own up to them:* No one said role models have to be 100 percent perfect. There is no Mary Poppins (practically perfect) when it comes to role models. The most important part of this tip is that you *can* make a mistake, but you have to make sure you take responsibility. As a role model, your accountability sets an example for all to see and then practice.

Question 158. What Are the Golden Rules for Modern Communicators?

I remember one of my mentors giving me sage advice when I started in PR. He said, "If you listen, then you will do well." The same still holds true today. Whether you are physically meeting with your customers or you are "listening" or monitoring conversations online and through social media, listening will help you to solve challenges, build relationships, and grow as a professional. Listening is always my number one rule that I pass along to all the professionals and students that I mentor today.

However, there are many golden rules when you're a modern communicator. Here are some of my favorite rules that have influenced my decisions over the past 25+ years:

- Don't just say the right thing, but do the right thing. Actions speak louder than words.
- At the end of the day, the only thing you have left is your integrity and this should not be compromised.

- A handful of great relationships is better than a lengthy list of okay connections.
- Always connect business and communications; pinpoint how what you do will directly impact and create value for your organization.
- Give back to the industry that has educated you by mentoring younger professionals.
- Practice PR as if it also stands for Proactive Relations and Personal Relationships.

You will develop your own golden rules over the years. However, no matter how the career landscape changes and technology continues to advance your connections, these golden rules are timeless.

Of course, there is one last rule that we can't forget … Don't do as I say, but rather do as I do, which makes it really important that you are subscribing to all of these golden rules.

The Experts Weigh In

Aliza Licht, Founder and CEO of Leave Your Mark, author of *Leave Your Mark*

Pay It Forward

People always emphasize the importance of remembering where you came from. For the most part, people do, they just sometimes forget all the people along the way who made their future possible.

Experiencing success and failure is like getting a Harvard education. It's a gift and one that requires sharing. If you can learn from someone's mistakes, why shouldn't you? Good karma is good business. In the same vein, if you can pave the way for someone to have an easier time than you did, you should. Some people believe that they are somehow keeping a competitive edge by hoarding connections or not sharing information. They're not. Being an uber-connector makes you valuable to your network. Being someone who is willing to answer a few questions or give a piece of advice makes you all the more powerful. Being a mentor isn't only about handholding, it can also be about wrist slapping. To pay it forward is to lead the way and real leaders are never afraid of the people who walk behind them. Real leaders are too busy looking ahead to the future to care.

Gail Nelson, Head of Marketing, SYZYGY

On Giving Back as a Mentor

I had an amazing mentor at my first job. He taught me more than just what I needed to know to do the work: he explained the ways of business and the whys behind the forces driving our industry. He even listened to my ideas, as naïve as they often were. Without his mentorship, I would have had a much harder time making the transition from college graduate to productive business person.

I've tried to follow his example. While the business world has certainly changed, investing time and energy in your fellow workers makes as much sense as it always has.

The young people I know today who are looking to build a marketing career typically have (or quickly polish) marketable skills such as writing, analytics, and marketing campaign automation. Where they struggle is decoding the underlying mix of cultural norms and human foibles that drive the (dis)function of the workplace. A thoughtful mentor can also help young professionals accurately assess their strengths and potential career paths and identify when it's time to seek opportunity at a new employer or in graduate school.

One talented young woman, whom I know had notched two years of work experience, showed real leadership potential. I believed she could learn a lot in a sales role and would excel there. She was tenacious, goal-driven, a top-notch communicator, and unafraid to engage senior people. But she was worried about trying out a business development role for myriad reasons, including concerns about being "just a salesperson." She came to understand sales success can bring status and, at minimum, what she learns in a sales role can help make her become a more effective B2B marketing leader, if that's where she chooses to take her career.

I don't believe this young woman will outgrow her need for mentorship any more than I have. The term "mentor" doesn't only define the relationship between a younger and an older worker. In my experience, it's a way of interacting with fellow professionals throughout your working life. Mid- and late-career people need objective perspectives and support as they navigate job disruptions, their own changing perspectives on work, and shifting definitions of a happy life. My advice to careerists of all ages is twofold: Be a mentor; get a mentor.

Wendy Glavin, CEO, Wendy Glavin Agency

People of All Ages Need Mentoring

When I was young, my attorney father was my mentor. Like any skilled prosecutor, his teachings were always around proving arguments, "beyond a reasonable doubt." To illustrate, he used the classic children's story, *The Three Little Pigs* and asked me to argue each pig's case and the wolf's case. It taught me there are different sides to a story.

When I was older, we watched movies and discussed their meaning. *To Kill a Mockingbird* was acting with moral courage. *Twelve Angry Men* shows how using rational argument and persuasion can overcome bias and prejudice. *Inherit the Wind* exemplifies the right to freedom of thought.

Throughout my life, I've had mentors. While transitioning from corporate to agency work, the head of public relations taught me how to improve my writing. Through reading, research, and surrounding myself with different people and ideas, I developed abstract thinking.

Twenty years ago, I met a Parisian woman, my next mentor. Through her, my family was afforded the luxury of living in the south of France. While there, being immersed in a different culture, surrounded by sunflowers and chateaux, markets bustling with food, clothing and accessories, different colors, smells, and a slower way of life, broadened me like no other experience.

That is until I had my three boys and viewed life from a young person's perspective to better understand them. I played basketball and baseball, read and learned about their much-loved books, authors and playwrights, Dr. Seuss, Roald Dahl, and Redwall. When they were older, favorites were Shakespeare's *Othello, Paradise Lost*, and *Life of Pi*. I mentored them by example with honesty, strength, and unconditional love. Today, they are my role models.

Now, I mentor students at colleges and events, like the Girl Scouts Pitch Fest (teams of girls pitching apps). Before presentations, I send a 20-question anonymous survey to learn about my audience. Many students are confused about the differences between the marketing, public relations, and advertising professions.

Interactive presentations work best, as does jokingly threatening to call on them if they don't ask or answer questions. Receiving a round of applause from a group of 25 college students and having a student say, "Ms. Glavin, your presentation was awesome," is awesome!

I disagree about Millennial assumptions. I've met and helped so many and am amazed how open, curious, and grateful they are to receive help and advice. A number of students have even asked me out for coffee or lunch. I've always been outgoing, but at 20, I doubt I would have had the guts to ask a guest speaker out for a meal.

People of all ages need mentoring. Young people can learn from older people about different professions, or what personality traits work best for some professions, while older people can learn from younger people about Instagram, Snap Chat, and the best online services, such as Venmo.

Last November, I was in a taxi that crashed with a Mack truck. Laid-up for three months, I needed my website to generate leads, rather than just being an online presence.

After participating in Deirdre Breakenridge's #PRSTUDCHAT, watching her podcasts and following her online, I reached out. I explained what happened to me and asked, "With so many lead generation tools, which would you suggest?"

Several emails later, I decided Deirdre could help me overcome my challenge. Her weekly coaching sessions offer so many things: Empathy, strategic vision, humility, passion, inspiration, and unending support.

Deirdre exemplifies, "I want to inspire people. I want someone to look at me and say, because of you I didn't give up."

Note

1 Women Worldwide Podcast, "The Best Ways to Create Pride of Ownership and Inspire Innovation with Jane Boyce," February 10, 2017.

Chapter 8

Advancing with More Questions, Answers, and Opportunities

Even after you have reviewed all of the questions and answers presented, there will be so many more to come. If you think about it, asking and answering questions is the job of the modern communicator. That is the nature of your role: to be curious and learn as much as you can. At the same time, being a modern communicator also means you are the problem solver. You need to have answers very quickly, whether they are for your leadership team or the public you serve. The modern communicator has to find the careful balance between constant learning and embracing what is new and what is next.

Who is the modern communicator? You are, of course. But, there is always room to sharpen your skills and to communicate more effectively. Actually, anyone in business, working with a business, or working at a business, needs to communicate effectively. Consumer behavior and new technologies are driving monumental changes with every passing day. Navigating these important changes in behavior and understanding the evolving media landscape will certainly require asking and answering many more important questions throughout your career.

Modern communicators play a unique role that no one else can fill. You have to be prepared for the opportunities and challenges of everyday businesses operating in a global environment. Whether your business is local or actually global, communication transcends borders and geographical boundaries. You have to be universal in your thinking, focusing on diversity and being completely flexible and adaptable in an ever-changing landscape—the exact reason why you have to learn the essentials of good communication, no matter what kind training you receive. What you share internally and publicly will always have consequences. Yes, words through any channel still have meaning and, at times, repercussions. The speed of technology and a dynamic public make this our new reality.

As a modern communicator, learning the essential lessons and practicing them are the only ways to move forward. Regardless of the changes in technology, media, and consumer behavior, it will be your core principles that guide you. Ethics, trust, accuracy, accountability, reliability, honesty, etc., should be at the top of your priority list. At the end of the day, when you are done communicating, you are left with your own integrity. Your future in communications will require you to say the right thing, and also do the right thing to keep your credibility intact. Looking ahead 10, 20 or even 30 years from now, this will not change.

Relationships should always be at the cornerstone of your communication. You will continue to find new ways to connect with people, engage in different communities, and grow your relationships on a deeper level. Facebook, Twitter, Snapchat, and Instagram in 2017, but who knows the communities and the technology of the future. Regardless of the technology, the future of your relationships will be based on what your "friends" have experienced with you and what they expect from you. Your role in the friendship is genuine when your bond comes from a place of intense listening, learning, and understanding. Always uphold and reinforce what initially brought you together and you will naturally increase the strength of your connection over time.

Were there ever situations in the past when you've said, "Why didn't I keep in touch?" When you experience that initial important connection, you can't take this for granted. Don't wait for your new acquaintance to make a move. The modern communicator realizes there are no excuses when it comes to fostering new relationships and making good relationships last for the long term. Social media has taught us that we can always connect, share, and strengthen our bonds anytime and anywhere in the world.

Modern communicators also identify how friends fall into different kinds of relationship buckets. There is nothing wrong with knowing the "buckets" where your friends reside and the best ways to help one another. Some of your relationships are built on business, and, very often, after the business relationship ends the friendship may wane. Then, there are those connections that follow you throughout a career and your lifetime. Both case scenarios are very important and serve a purpose. However, the latter, who are the lifetime career friends and mentors, are the folks who choose to follow you online and offline and grow with you over time. Modern communicators recognize the seeds of a great relationship. They work very hard to create opportunities with their friends and colleagues to collaborate and learn together. Along the way, they also connect others to do the same.

Your social media participation plays a tremendous role in your interactions and is one of the best ways to share compelling stories. Social media helps the modern communicator to discuss, learn, and embrace all that is modern in technology. Modern communicators are born tech testers who explore social media and mobile technologies: Augmented Reality (AR), Virtual Reality (VR), the Internet of Things (IoT), machine learning, and all that is new or on the horizon in our communications world. There is no sitting back to watch what everyone else is doing. Yes, you always have to be doing your research and learning new methods of communication to captivate your audiences.

But, the real opportunity and value comes in the form of applying yourself and pushing the technology envelope. I remember a former agency employee saying that he was leaving my firm because of the technology we used. Our progress in tech was too intimidating. He said, "I want to finish familiar," meaning he was going to end his career on a familiar note. The modern communicator cannot and will not finish familiar.

New learning is around every corner and technology makes it incredibly easy. For every single person who says, "I don't get social media" or "I don't think I need to be socializing my brand," to be a modern communicator, I encourage you to step back and rethink your progress and growth. You have to be social and learn the new ways to communicate to keep up with your peers, savvy consumers, and business constituents.

At the same time, any communicator who says, "I know everything," can't possibly know everything! If this is the case, then you are not pushing yourself to learn more and you can welcome yourself to the "status quo." If you are always the smartest person in the room, then you are hanging out in the wrong rooms and circles. How do you learn, grow, and challenge yourself to excel when you know everything? This is your time to rethink how social media and technology can change your mindset. And, if you change your thinking, then you'll also be able to increase your opportunity.

Of course, one of your biggest areas of focus is content. Yes, content is both king and queen and rules the media landscape, although distribution is incredibly important. If you can't figure out where to reach your audience, then why bother creating the content? Of course, you should challenge yourself to perfect your strategic storytelling approach, and the way you develop and share your compelling information. However, the only way to truly understand what people want from you is to involve them in your content initiatives and the building of their favorite brands. The companies and the professionals who have mastered the art of crowdsourcing or co-creating are the best at understanding how people want to engage. The best brands of the future will be in the hands of the people they serve. Their modern communicators will be there every step of the way to shape and guide those interactions.

As you are learning to ramp up your stories, mastering the art of modern communication, you are also opening up the social media flood gates. There is no taking back what you say. The do-over doesn't exist. Because perception is different for everyone and you know the potential reach of a social network, you have to be committed to and focused on your brand. Reputation is a function of what you say and also what you do. It takes years to raise a child, and, yes, it takes a village. Like a reputation, it takes time, and an army of champions, as you are building brand equity. The trust bank grows if you are watching, listening carefully, and saying and doing the right things.

However, even the best brands face negative situations and crises, which can have a deep effect on how people feel and whether they remain loyal to you. Brands make missteps all of the time. The damage is a direct reflection of how they handle themselves before, during, and after a tough situation. If your "good will" cup is full beforehand, then you will have advocates to help you. Of course, if you don't communicate with authenticity, accuracy, and honesty, well, that cup will spill right over. As a modern communicator, you know the importance of a healthy brand. You will be building, maintaining, and protecting the life of your brands by thinking AHEAD to guide your communications, while you build trust through transparency.

How does the modern communicator show accountability? Accountability and the "tangible" have been a challenge for years. But here is the good news: You know the rules of modern communication measurement. No more fairy dust and—poof!—there is value. Proving business value takes work, including detailed plans with precise goals and objectives. The science part of your role is just as important as the art or your storytelling. The biggest lessons regarding measurement start with expectations and are based on performance. Yes, these are the tangibles you can track. In the online and social media world, this means from click to conversion. How can you demonstrate this value? Although there are executives who still want to see the vanity metrics such as thousands of likes and views, you know better.

The modern communicator also knows that the Advertising Value Equivalency (AVE) is not a measurement option. AVE should stand for Absolute *Valueless* Equivalency; the unmotivated professional's measurement. Accountability is hard work because you have to track and trace, bringing the pieces of the impact puzzle together. But don't just take my advice; other experts have weighed in too. If you are truly a modern communicator, then you will be pushing your data literacy limits and taking a deep dive into different data sets to show how all the pieces of the marketing Return on Investment (ROI) puzzle fit together. From this point forward, get out of your silo to collaborate with other communication professionals as well as your internal sales, customer service, HR, research, and product development partners. Integrated on the inside is one of the best ways to show how the results of your program go across the organization and how, together, you are reaching your company's higher-level goals.

Social media offers the opportunity to learn in many different communities, whether it is with your communications colleagues or professionals outside of your industry. People are communicating through online courses, forums, tweet chats, blogs, and the list goes on. Do you realize that every time you create a blog or publish to LinkedIn, post a thoughtful comment in a Facebook group or create a video on a pressing topic, you are mentoring someone? When you are participating in a Twitter chat and you are answering questions as a community, the entire community is learning. You are helping your professional peers. There are times you will pursue formal mentor/mentee relationships. But if you want to keep up with a giving spirit and a pay-it-forward attitude, then, by all means, use social media as a way to share information, insights, and advice with your younger peers. Remember, no one will remind you when to become a mentor and to start answering questions. You'll know when you are ready and your peers will thank you.

The role of the professional communicator stands out now and will stand out as an even more important role as communication and technology continue to evolve. From the new start ups and entrepreneurial ventures to corporate communications and non-profit fundraising, your communication carries a tremendous amount of weight and relevance for an organization. Regardless of your title or years in your field, it is the landscape and the people that shape your activities as a modern communicator. When you embrace the technology to drive deeper engagement, you can make a difference. Despite the incredible pace of technology, vastly changing platforms and the new behaviors that ensue, there are still a few "sure bets" you can make. History helps you to understand, reflect, and move forward. Your own experience and learning through the experience of others will help to keep you on the right path. At the same time, technology and the instantaneous feedback from your customers will also help you to adjust your communication in real time.

As you venture forward, don't hold back with your questions or your answers. In the past, maybe you didn't feel as if you had the right place to offer insights or you didn't have a source who inquired. Well, now you have an open invitation to ask a question and share your thoughts as a modern communicator. I'll be listening, along with many of my colleagues in the industry. You can find me on Twitter—I'm @dbreakenridge; connect to me on LinkedIn or you can email me directly at Deirdre@PurePerformanceComm.com.

You can also join any number of groups or communities on LinkedIn, Twitter, Facebook, or Google+ and your professional peers will be happy to answer your questions. But get ready … they may have some questions for you. We live in a world where everyone has questions and everyone wants to communicate. Social media and your natural ability as a modern communicator prompts you to help someone else.

I believe the modern communicator can't resist helping, sharing, and communicating; it is in your DNA. You were born a listener, problem solver, and mentor. Now, you can take everything you have learned from the pages of this book to answer more questions on your own.

Are you ready for more learning, pressing questions, sharing information, and communicating on a whole new level? Moving forward, your gift to your professional peers and the businesses you serve comes in the form of the questions you pose and the answers you provide.

Good luck on your journey as a modern communicator. I hope you will move along your path, asking and answering questions and finding incredible opportunities for your continued success in the years ahead.

Index